ELECTRIC VEHICLES

What About Them?!?

by Richard Rosenthal

Richard P. Rosenthal

Welcome to our future!

Other books by the author:

The Murder of Old Comrades

Sky Cops

K-9 Cops

Rookie Cop, Deep Undercover in the JDL (Jewish Defense League)

Practical Handgun Training

Self-Publishing~Simplified!

Nogales, Sasabe, Lochiel~ Part of our Third Nation

Use of Force in Modern Policing

Groundhog Day...

Reincarnation and the Near-Death Experience~ A Secular View

Copyright © 2023 by Richard P. Rosenthal, Publisher

Eighth Edition

This book is protected by copyright. No part of it may be reproduced in any manner without written permission from the publisher.

Available from: ***Amazon***

Contact the author at: *RichWellfleet@Comcast.net*

Electric Vehicles, What About Them?!?

Note about book "Editions"

As the electric vehicle world is changing so rapidly; with new vehicles becoming available, software changes, additional range and charging speed testing, charging infrastructure growth and modifications, etc., I try to put out a "new" book edition around every six months. I do not wish to imply remarkable sales numbers of this book with the number of editions shown (this latest being the sixth), just simply that this is my way to ensure a clear differentiation between the various updated versions.

Table of Contents

Abbreviations *6*
Disruptive Technologies *8*
What Exactly is an Electric Vehicle?? A Bit of History *17*
Some Things You Should Know About EVs *39*
Distance Travel by EV?~Read This First!! *72*
Boring Stuff *80*
A Preface to the Next Chapter on new EVs Expected to Come on the Market Soon *83*
Some EVs~Cars and Pickups~ Here Now or On the Horizon *84*
Apps and Maps *100*
Tesla *116*
Magic Dock!! *123*
Electrify America (EA) Charging App *125*
Where Is This All Heading?? *132*
How to Road-Trip in an EV! *135*
Places to Go for More Information *144*
Tested Ranges of Assorted EVs *152*
Charging Speeds of Various EVs *161*
Road Trips We've Taken *164*
Arizona to Cape Cod~Tesla Model Y ~2842 Miles (May 2023) *165*
Cape Cod to AZ to Pick-Up a Tesla Model 3 SR LFP ~2925 Miles (August 2022) *168*

Arizona to Cape Cod~Tesla Model Y~2800 Miles Using a Tesla CCS Adapter!! (June 2022) *175*

Cape Cod to Arizona~ 3,435 Miles in our Tesla Model Y (October 2021) *179*

Another Cross-Country EV Trip ~ 2,861 Miles in a Tesla Model Y (April 2021) *185*

A Long EV Trip ~ 2,742 Miles in a Chevrolet Bolt (October 2020) *190*

Thank You Note to My "Staff" *203*

Abbreviations

Too often I have seen explanations of the meaning of abbreviations used in books placed at the very end of the work. My thought is readers truly need them before starting on reading text containing unfamiliar material!

General/Common Terms

EV   Electric Vehicle

BEV   Battery Electric Vehicle
(same type vehicle as an *EV*)

HEV   Hybrid Electric Vehicle (generally, a vehicle with no option to plug in for charging the on-board traction battery)

PHEV Plug-in Hybrid Electric Vehicle

AC   Alternate Current

AFC   Alternate Fuel Vehicle (perhaps one using a biofuel)

DC   Direct Current
(as used in an *EV* traction battery or drive battery)

DCFC Direct Current Fast Charger. *DCFC* stations are springing up around the nation.

FCV   Fuel Cell Vehicle (most often hydrogen)

GOM "Guess-O-Meter" (*EV* humor) or estimated mileage gauge

ICE   Internal Combustion Engine
(a "normal" gasoline/diesel fuel auto)

NEMA National Electrical Manufacturer Association. Most often seen in this book to describe electrical plug configurations
(such as NEMA 14-50, or NEMA 5-20)

OEM Original Equipment Manufacturer. Most often referring to auto manufacturers such as Ford, GM, VW, Tesla, etc.

SoC   State of Charge (of the traction battery)

Electric Vehicles, What About Them?!?

ZEV   Zero Emission Vehicle (such as one using hydrogen for its fuel cell, or an *EV*)

Types of Charging "Plugs"

J1772	Common plug used in North and South America for "normal" (not fast charge speed) *EV* charging.
CCS1	Combined Charging System. Used for fast charging in the United States, Canada and Mexico (Europe uses CCS2 type). Most common for *EVs* here except for Tesla models (which uses a propriety shaped plug, which actually came first).
CHAdeMO	Seen in only a few *EVs* in the United States. Used mostly in Europe, Japan as well as other Asian nations.
EVSE	Electric Vehicle Supply Equipment (an *EV's* "charger" unit. The "box" and cord attached to the electric outlet connecting to your *EV*).
Supercharger	A term coined by Tesla for their fast-charging stations. These plugs have the same basic plug configuration as their "normal" charge plug.
DCFC	Direct Current Fast Chargers. Most common non-Tesla system.
Tesla Destination Chargers	Level 2 chargers found at motels and restaurants for use by Tesla *EVs*.

EV plug types (Receiving end)

7

Richard P. Rosenthal

Disruptive Technologies

or

"I thought we were just going to talk about cars?"

By 2030 it is likely you will be hard pressed to find a newly manufactured internal combustion engine (*ICE*) personal transportation vehicle for sale (be it a car, small truck, two or three wheeled vehicle). The reason has little to do with "saving the planet" but will be far more likely the result of simple economics and advances in technology. You will have by then concluded that electric vehicles (*EVs*) are less expensive to buy, own, as well as to operate and maintain than the older technology (and soon, basically obsolete) hydrocarbon (gasoline or diesel) powered models of vehicle.

Electric Vehicles, or *EVs*, are part of a wider number of disruptive technological developments which are coming to fruition just about now and which we will see becoming popular in the near future.

Tony Seba, a gentleman who I shall refer to as a future strategist argues that with *EVs* we are seeing one of series of "disruptive technologies" now taking place in the world. A disruptive technology is defined as both changing how "things" are done, while at the same time sweeping away the system which preceded these changes. Thus, a new market is created while destroying or significantly diminishing the older existing one.

Jobs are lost. Jobs are created. Just ask the Luddites![*]

[*]A member of any of the bands of English workers who destroyed the then newly invented milling machinery, especially in cotton and woolen mills, which they believed was threatening their jobs (1811~1816).

Some years ago, someone from one of the OPEC (oil producing) Arab nations was asked why his nation was investing in alternate sources of energy while sitting on an ocean of petroleum? He was quoted as responding; "The stone age did not end because people ran out of stones."

Nor will the use of *ICE* vehicles come to an end because we have run out of petroleum. They will simply be replaced by superior as well as less expensive products.

Luddites destroying a milling machine. It didn't stop progress.

We will all change over to *EVs* when the cost of using other sources of energy to power our vehicles becomes increasingly more expensive than electricity. I suggest this will happen with a rapidity which will surprise us all. This is not some bright idea I've come up with (as I have run out of bright ideas some years ago…), but the opinion of Tony Seba, which he presents in a data-rich video on the subject;

The Collapse of the Oil, Coal & ICE Vehicle Industries
https://www.youtube.com/watch?v=O-kbzfWzvSI

Seba states that in a few years (a decade perhaps) the economics of using petroleum for assorted energy generation (electrical, transport, whatever purpose) will simply be more expensive than the energy available for this purpose in the renewable sector. This changeover will not take place because people are desiring to save the planet, wish to enhance air quality or any of the myriad other reasons some folks aspire to make this happen in order for such a transition to occur. The change will come as a natural result of lower costs for one type of energy over another. In other words, self-interest will prevail.

Consider this; horses were a major means of transportation for thousands of years. Tony Seba informs us that in 1894 the following observation in praise of this means of transport was made:

"(*Horses are*) self-feeding, self-controlling, self-maintaining and self-reproducing, but they are far more economical in the energy they are able to develop from a given weight of fuel material, than any other existing form of motor." (Nikiforuk, 2013)

New York City 1894

As with horses, petroleum will not completely disappear. For over a hundred years we have used *ICE* vehicles to get around, yet horses still exist. These animals, used for thousands of years, are simply impractical for use today (slow and quite expensive) for transportation. At the turn of the 19th into the 20th century, when autos and trucks replaced these beasts, what did we do with the now

Electric Vehicles, What About Them?!?

overabundance of horses? According to Tony Seba we used them for recreation, ate them, or turned them into dog food.

Keep in mind when this changeover took place people lost jobs. Without large numbers of these animals to service, stable owners, feed producers, trainers, horse veterinarians, road cleaners etc., became obsolete and went out of business.

None the less, even today you can still use a horse in order to move around. It will be slow travel, inconvenient, and rather pricy, but it can be done.

In his book, *Rethinking Humanity*, Seba wrote that;

"The Ford Model T, introduced in 1908, had a power-to-weight ratio 54 times higher than the 1885 Otto *ICE* and cost $825 (about $41 per horsepower). At the time, the price of a carriage and two (low end) horses was around $820 (about $410 per horsepower), meaning the Model T price/performance was 10X that of the leading mainstream mode of transportation."

New York City 1913

Seba went on to state what is evident; the Model T was faster, could carry more cargo, and could travel further in a day than any horse-drawn mode of transport. In short, it was a superior technology.

According to Seba, the move from animal to machine transport took about twenty years to accomplish. He points out in the video (and in his book) that it was interesting to note that in about ten years' time w1894as when was seen the initial surge in this transition from animal powered to machine enabled mobility;

11% internal combustion vehicle propulsion was in use in 1910. This rose to 81% motorized vehicle use by 1920!

That is because as a disruptive technology (as in any new technological adoption) the switchover came in the form of an "S" curve. He states this is the norm and is <u>always</u> how disruptive technologies have been seen to increase in their effect and adoption within a society.

New York City 5th Avenue Buses 1913

Seba points out that the auto disruption came about in that ten-year period in spite of:

> ➢ Our needing to build several industries; auto manufacture as well as both oil production and refining facilities

Electric Vehicles, What About Them?!?

- The United States was fighting in a major war (WWI)
- The nation needed to build a new road and fueling infrastructure to accommodate the new vehicles
- Our having to deal with an influenza pandemic!

Seba also points out that it is the people most involved in the current "normal" technology being displaced who are invariably the last to recognize the quickly shifting sands. He also suggests that when such people try and evaluate what the future holds, they are mostly wrong.

My personal favorite quote, which describes this phenomenon, is from Upton Sinclair;

"It is difficult for a man to know something when his salary depends on his not knowing it."

One example Seba uses to portray how such a mind-set plays out was when in 1985 ATT asked a "think tank" to calculate how many cell phones would be in use by the year 2000 (then just fifteen years into their future). ATT was attempting at the time to figure out the potential market for such a product.

The answer which came back after the research was completed was a prediction that 900,000 such phones would be in use fifteen years into their future. The actual number, in 2000, turned out to be **_109 million!_**

In order for a disruptive technology to come to fruition (actually, for it to even exist) several factors (inventions, technologies, discoveries) must occur at the same proximate time. For cell phones it was computer chip power, data storage, network capacity, Li-ion batteries, touchscreens, sensors, and GPS. Some guys put it all together, called the devices Smartphones, and here we are! Remove just one or two of the elements from that mix and there goes our ubiquitous cell phone usage.

Energy

Coal is dead. Not because it's dirty (and it is), but due to the fact that this fuel is now too expensive for use as an energy source. Oil and nuclear will both soon be more expensive than renewables, and thus will slowly become obsolete for energy generation even as I'm writing this. By around 2025 oil as a primary source of energy will be severely negatively impacted by the upcoming disruptive technologies. This is a fact, not some fanciful, tin-foil hat rant on my part. Tony Seba lays out this argument in far greater detail in his books and videos than I am able, backed up by hard data.

Only a few months ago, for a period of time, oil went negative in cost. The writing is on the wall. Demand will eventually dry up. Oil will be too expensive to get out of the ground, process, transport, and store. It's just a matter of cost. Period.

Our existing grid is extremely inefficient. Batteries will eventually replace central power generation as the primary source for most of our energy storage needs. This has already taken place in some parts of the world; Australia and England are two locations where such a change has occurred.

Computing Power

I'm just going to touch on this aspect of the ongoing disruption. In 2000 a TeraFlop[*] of computer memory cost $46 million dollars (Seba). The computer using this enormous memory system required 1,600 sq. ft. of space, and power consumption was significant.

[*] A teraflop refers to the capability of a processor to calculate one trillion floating-point operations per second. Saying something has "5 TFLOPS," for example, means that its processor setup is capable of handling 5 trillion floating-point calculations every second, on average.

In 2015 you could buy eight TFlops of memory for $600. Power consumption was low, and the device could be held in your hands. The cost for even more memory is far less today. Five TFlops comes built into the Apple 10 for the cost of buying the device.

You need such levels of computer memory in order for self-driving cars (really all modes of transport which moves autonomously, without human interaction) in order for such vehicles to be a viable useable technology. Hundreds of TFlops.

Electric Vehicles, What About Them?!?

<u>Vehicles</u>

My wife and I owned a 2019 Chevrolet Bolt (turned it back into Chevy and bought a Tesla model 3) and a Tesla model Y *EV*. All three are pure *EVs*. The Bolt is a wonderful small car, reliable, remarkably nimble, fast, well made, and was practical for my wife's and my personal transportation purposes. The Bolt is already outdated for road-trips (it fast-charges much too slowly), as the advances in the field are simply moving so rapidly. We recently purchased the Tesla Model Y for distance travel (+10,000 road-trip miles to date). We also own a Jeep Wrangler, a fun little *ICE* machine. None the less, we see a time in a few years when we will no longer own any *ICE* vehicles.

The convergence of several technologies will be highly disruptive to both our society's energy use as well as how we will transport people and things. Among these changes will be:

- Batteries (costs will trend down while energy density will increase)
- Electric Vehicles (*EV*) will be widely adopted
- Autonomous vehicles will become the norm
- On-Demand transport will replace personally owned vehicles
- Solar energy generation will majorly impact centralized energy generation plants

Batteries for *EVs* are heading (very probably are there now*) toward a useful life of over one million road miles, with an ever-increasing energy density, all the while at a falling cost. "People" do not need a million-mile battery, but fleet owners do. It would take the average car owner perhaps twenty or more years to "use up" a million-mile battery. A fleet owner might find the useful life of such an energy source to be around five years. All the while at a cost of under 1/3 the expenditure when compared to an otherwise identical *ICE* vehicle.

*Tesla has recently announced their 4680 battery cell. This cell chemistry and configuration may well have a real-world life span of around two million road miles. The battery pack will likely be moved from one *EV* body to a newer one as the "shell" of the older vehicle is worn out.

Thus a fleet owner can buy one *EV* van or taxi for five or ten years of use or three or four *ICE* cars/vans for the same period of time. And if using the new Tesla 4680 battery, when their old fleet vehicle is worn out, the battery from that unit can then be put into its replacement. Such a decision will simply be a matter of economics, having little or nothing to do with "saving the planet."

Based on the lowering of *EV* costs which will be required to purchase and operate such machines, by sometime around 2025 it will not make any economic sense to buy a new *ICE* vehicle.

New car *ICE* sales are falling and will continue to do so. The United States vehicle fleet will shrink, according to Seba, by 80% by 2030. Sometime around 2030 most people will not even bother owning a car but will use on-call autopilot-controlled vehicles for their normal transport needs.

Once again, it is simply a matter of economics.

Much the same calculation comes to play when considering what we will be utilizing for home energy use in the future. The inexorable answer is, renewable energy (my guess it being generated by solar arrays; which are increasingly cheap, easy to install, and effective). This change has nothing to do with concern over the well-being for the world's population, rising sea levels or any other issue. It is just a matter of self-interest and money.

Relax, enjoy the ride, it will be an exciting one!

*

Electric Vehicles, What About Them?!?

What Exactly is an Electric Vehicle?? A Bit of History

"Mmmm, fire, good!"
Comment attributed to an early *Homo sapien* inventor who developed the means to cook food and heat dwellings.
No one in his tribe thought the idea would ever catch on.

Well, for one thing modern electric vehicles (*EVs*) are not simply little golf-cart like contraptions (well, it is true that golf-carts are mostly electric, but such limited use vehicles are not what this book is all about!). These are serious, technically superior personal transportation vehicles, which are rapidly turning machines utilizing internal combustion engines (*ICE*) obsolete.

We are speaking here of autos which you can jump into in Los Angeles and a few days later pull into New York City, with a minimum of fuss and bother. An automobile which will likely have greater acceleration than virtually any other non-electric car on the road around you, which will be very quiet, extraordinarily reliable and most important of all, extremely cost effective to own and operate.

Let us start at the beginning.

<u>The Electric Vehicle (*EV*)</u>

EVs (electric vehicles) are not new. These machines have been around for well over a hundred years. In November 1881, Gustave Trouvé presented an electric car he designed at the Exposition Internationale d'Électricité de Paris. Trouvé fitted an electric motor, a type which he had improved upon, to a tricycle, put a rechargable battery on the machine, and thus invented the world's first *EV*! For reasons I could not discover Monsieur Trouvé was unable to obtain a patent on his device. A prolific inventor, the man also invented a motor used in marine applications, thus also being credited as the person who invented the outboard engine!

In 1884 an Englishman, Thomas Parker, built a larger, somewhat more practical *EV* in Wolverhampton. Please see the included photo of his vehicle, which was taken in 1895.

Fig. 13: Tricycle électrique de Trouvé
(Alexis Clerc, *Physique et chimie populaires*, vol. 2, 1881-1883).

Gustave Trouvé and his electric vehicle!

Henry Ford's wife, Clara, preferred her Detroit Electric car to her husband's products for her personal transportation use. Henry purchased her a new *EV* each year (or every two years, I have read assertions of both being the correct number) from 1908 until 1914.

Her Detroit Electric could do eighty (80) miles on a charge and had a top speed of twenty (20) miles an hour. Keep in mind the marginal condition of the roads at the turn of the 19th into the 20th century, as well as the speeds normally seen by users when traveling in a horse-drawn carriage. Thus her vehicle was a very practical means of personal transport in her day.

It is interesting to note that both Henry Ford and Thomas Edison were interested in *EVs*.

Electric Vehicles, What About Them?!?

In the January 11, 1914 issue of the *New York Times* Henry Ford was quoted as stating:

"Within a year, I hope, we shall begin the manufacture of an electric automobile. I don't like to talk about things which are a year ahead, but I am willing to tell you something of my plans.

The fact is that Mr. Edison and I have been working for some years on an electric automobile which would be cheap and practicable. Cars have been built for experimental purposes, and we are satisfied now that the way is clear to success. The problem so far has been to build a storage battery of lightweight which would operate for long distances without recharging. Mr. Edison has been experimenting with such a battery for some time."

Thomas Edison was a fan of the electric car as well. He stated:

"Electricity is the thing. There are no whirring and grinding gears with their numerous levers to confuse. There is not that almost terrifying uncertain throb and whirr of the powerful combustion engine. There is no water circulating system to get out of order – no dangerous and evil-smelling gasoline and no noise."

While both Ford and Edison worked on developing a practical *EV* they didn't succeed.

In 1914 a Detroit Electric went 241 miles on a single charge setting a new record! Its top speed was 25 MPH. None the less, considering the quality of the roads back then that was quite a feat.

Edison Next to EV of His

According to Jay Leno, when discussing electric autos (specifically the Baker models) during this early period, he stated; "There were thousands of these (Baker *EVs*) in New York (City), from about 1905 to 1915. There were charging stations all over town, so ladies could recharge their cars while they were in the stores."

A Parker EV around 1895

Jay muses that one of the reasons the early *EVs* did not prevail in the market was that men were uncomfortable driving a "woman's car." Silly, but I have seen similar situations. I spent forty-one years as a police officer, twenty of them in the NYPD. Without going into the minutia of the story the department had procured a well-thought-out compact revolver (a S&W model 36, in .38 Special) with a three-inch "heavy" barrel. It made for a far superior detective's handgun than the two-inch barrel revolvers then in vogue carried by detectives and plain clothed officers. Problem was, someone had given it the name of "Policewoman's gun" as one of the reasons for its existence was to replace the inadequate .32 S&W caliber revolvers women officers had been required to carry up to that time in the department's history.

Electric Vehicles, What About Them?!?

Because of the name few male officers ever purchased one! If only someone had thought to name the handgun the "Investigator Special!"

Back to the topic at hand. The advantage the electrically powered autos over gasoline powered vehicles had back then were numerous:

- They didn't blow up,
- They didn't break your arm when performing a crank-start (which could happen should the engine "kick-back." With an *EV*, just push a button or flip a switch to start! Once the Kettering electric self-starter became popularized in gasoline powered (*ICE*) autos this danger was eliminated.)
- No hard-to-obtain, smelly and explosive gasoline was needed to fuel the vehicles
- They were much cleaner to be around (again, no gasoline, oil, or radiator fluid was required)
- The machines were quiet
- They were simple to operate
- They were reliable

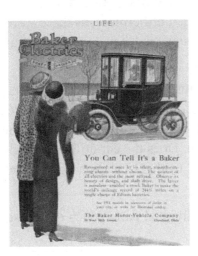

The then popular Baker Electric

A Detroit Electric as preferred by Clara Ford (Henry's wife)

Their modest speeds at that time in our history were no disadvantage. Indeed, some of the *EVs* of the period were developing speeds that matched their *ICE* rivals. Furthermore, as there were no interstate road systems in place these vehicles were perfectly suited for use in cities and towns.

There is a significant reduction in just the sheer number of parts making up the propulsion systems for an *EV* as opposed to an *ICE* vehicle. How many parts are there in an "normal" *ICE* auto? The actual number is tough to pin down. Does the car utilize an engine of; two cylinders? three? four? six? twelve? Turbocharged? Fuel injected? You get the idea.

The "best guess" number of the individual parts which comprise a typical auto engine is around 2,000.

Electric Vehicles, What About Them?!?

Keep in mind that such an engine consists of, among other components:

- ➢ Engine block plus sump, cylinder head, valve cover, inlet and exhaust manifolds
- ➢ Crankshaft and bearings
- ➢ Piston assembly: piston, rings, connecting rod and associated bearings
- ➢ Valve assembly: camshaft, valves, timing belt/chain, valve springs and various guides and bearings
- ➢ Ignition system (except for diesels): spark plugs, leads, coil pack
- ➢ Electronic: ECU and a variety of sensors, relays, and fuses
- ➢ Fuel system: low pressure pump, sender unit, high pressure pump, injector modules, fuel filters
- ➢ Auxiliaries: starter motor, alternator, water pump, oil pump, radiator, thermostat battery, oil filter, oil cooler
- ➢ Throttle body, air inlet hoses and filters

Such engines are large, heavy, and necessarily complex.

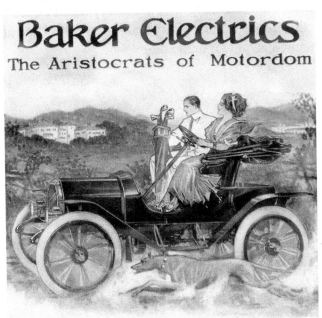

A Baker Electric. These were practical traveling machines in their day.

The *EV* Motor

The *EV* uses, need I say it, an electric motor, which is constructed of about twenty (20) parts. They are exceptionally reliable. When was the last time an electric fan motor in your home went kaput?!?

Please note the use of the term "motor" here, not engine. While I've seen the terms used interchangeably from time to time, I believe the preferred usage is to distinguish the internal combustion <u>engine</u> from the electric motor utilized in electric vehicles. Perhaps the definitions seen below can clear up the ambiguity.

> ➢ A motor is a machine that converts other forms of energy into mechanical energy and so imparts motion.
> ➢ An <u>engine</u> is a motor that converts thermal energy to mechanical work.

wordnetweb.princeton.edu

Still, people say outboard motor when speaking of a boat's engine, but you do not say an electric fan's engine, so there you are.

As you can see from the images of the two types of motors/engines the degree difference in complexity and size for the same amount of power generated is quite remarkable.

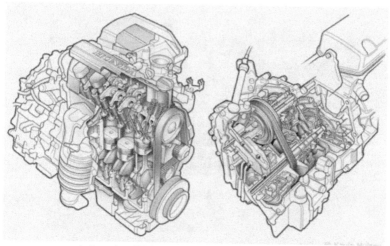

A "typical" internal combustion engine.

Electric Vehicles, What About Them?!?

The basic components of an *EV* (also referred to as a *BEV*, or Battery Electric Vehicle) are:

- ➤ Traction Battery Pack
- ➤ Electric Traction Motor
- ➤ Power Inverter
- ➤ Controller

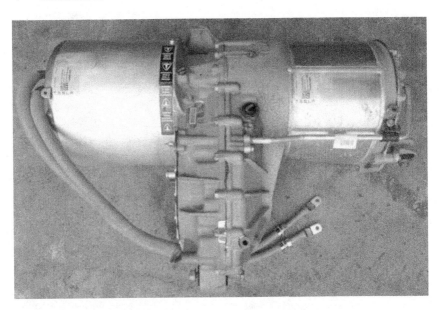

A Tesla model S motor

I have frequently read that an *EV* is basically an electric motor, a battery to supply energy to the motor, and a computer to figure the necessary interactions out needed to get the contraption to function.

The above shorthand explanation of the components of an *EV* is likely a bit too simplistic. Still, I hope it is of some use to you in your better understanding of these machines.

Traction Battery

This is where the electrical energy is stored, and used, for *EV* propulsion. These are direct current (DC) electrical components. Therefore fast chargers (used to "fill" these batteries as quickly as possible) are referred to as *DCFC* (Direct Current Fast Charging) stations.

Early traction battery. They would be flushed out and refilled with fresh acid after some use.

The actual design of these large and powerful banks of electrical storage batteries varies with the philosophies and end-goals of the assorted manufacturers. Tesla (and several other makers) use small cylindrically shaped cells which look remarkably like common "AA" or "D" size household batteries (they are somewhat larger however. The current Tesla iteration are known as 2170 cells, soon to be replaced with their very new 4680 batteries.).

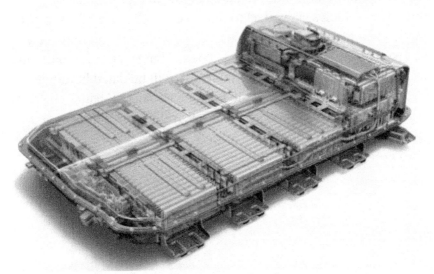

Chevy Bolt traction battery

A number of manufacturers utilize battery pouches for their vehicle's electrical energy storage form factor. The advantages and disadvantage of each type are carefully weighed by some really bright people in the field before deciding on which type of battery form ought to be used in their autos.

Considerations of which form is most suitable for their vehicles' use (and there are lots more than those I have mentioned below to consider, of that I'm sure) include:

- Specific energy of the individual cells
- Energy density
- Cell/pouch heating/cooling concerns
- Cost
- Cycle life
- Safety Issues

I doubt my readers would wish me to dive too deeply into the considerations given to the chemistry of *EV* batteries. Suffice it to say, this is a most complex, vibrant field of study. The main goal of the manufacturers is for the reduction in the cost of these batteries, whatever the format, in order to come below that of the cost of making *ICE* vehicles as well as to increase the *EV* duty life. Weight reduction is high on their list of "wants" as well. This all may well have taken place as I've penned this book. Things happen rapidly in this area. As I mentioned earlier, this book will be dated before it even goes to print! At any rate the most up to date *EV* batteries (Tesla 4680) have a lifespan of about one million road miles!

Pouch batteries compared to cell type versions

As an end user, your primary interests ought to revolve around (and this will be very dependent on your personal needs and desires) the cost of the *EV*, as well as the life expectancy of the batteries (which now routinely last in excess of 300,000 road miles and, as stated a moment earlier, will have better than one million miles of service life in the not-too-distant future!).

Keep in mind that all modern *EVs* now come with some sort of battery thermal management system (BTMS). Most batteries currently in use in *EVs* are "happiest" within a narrow temperature band, very roughly from 40°F/5°C to around 100°F/38°C, with 60°F/16°C to 80°F/27°C being the sweet spot.

Whether the *EV* you purchase uses the cell format or pouches, your primary concern should be that the traction battery of the vehicle is designed to receive all the necessary heating and cooling required to maintain battery health and long life. User reviews of any *EV* under consideration by you for purchase will likely have comments in regard any issues seen by those operating such cars.

Just a Few *EVs* Now Available or Which Soon Will Be

It would appear that there are several people claiming "their" electric car will be out soon, and its range, cost, speed, looks, smell (I jest) will outshine every other *EV* now on the market.

Maybe. For the moment let us take a look at just a few models which are either being sold right at this moment or which I am absolutely confident will be out shortly. In this chapter I will talk a bit about the Tesla company and their offerings. In the chapter titled; *Some Things You Should Know About EVs* we will look at other brands of *EVs* either available now or coming to market soon.

Tesla

Although other major manufacturers have either had *EVs* on the market (only to withdraw them) or are planning to introduce some in the very near future, this company, Tesla, was arguably the first to produce successful, practical, long range, fast and now affordable *EVs*, and to do so in significant numbers. The company's story is worth a moment of discussion time.

The first *EV* sold by Tesla was a unique sport vehicle, the Roadster. First out in 2008, this was a fast, long range (200 mile), lithium-ion battery cell powered, two seat *EV*. It was also quite expensive.

At the moment that vehicle is in orbit somewhere in our solar system (seriously. The vehicle was launched into space on February 6, 2018 on a *SpaceX* rocket.).

In 2012 the company came out with their model S. A luxury car, it was fast, comfortable, with decent range (now up to over 400 miles, soon to be ±500!) albeit pricey. A beautiful machine, but not for the masses.

Tesla 2012 model S

The model X first saw service in 2015. A large SUV, for whatever reason Tesla decided to design the car using gull-wing doors for the rear passengers. Large, comfortable, roomy, and expensive.

Finally, Tesla started to build *EVs* that "normal" people could hope to purchase. In 2017 came the model 3, a sporty four (five?) seater that was quick, with good range (to over 350 EPA miles depending on the model variant) and a solid practical traveling car. This vehicle can be had for about $50,000 dollars for the least expensive version (Standard Range using an LFP or iron/phosphate battery type).

Finally, and most recently (2020) Tesla has come out with the model Y. Looking like a model 3 that grew-up, this is a SUV (or "cross-over," whatever that means). This comfortable vehicle, suitable for distance travel, can carry around a good deal of "stuff" yet has excellent range (+300 miles, dependent on model), is fast, and, most important of all, relatively affordable. Price as of today starts in the +$60,000 range. My wife and I now own one for use as our distance *EV* travel vehicle. It is a very nice automobile.

Tesla 2020 model Y

This is the Tesla 4680 battery cell (46mmX80mm in dimension). Production for this style battery is just ramping up as this book is being written. The advantages of this cell will be increased useful life (a million road miles will be possible), the cells will hold energy more densely and they will be less expensive to manufacture than earlier type cells.

Tesla 4680 battery cell

Richard P. Rosenthal

Some Early EVs

Woods Electric.		**Woods Motor Vehicle Co., Chicago, Ill.**
PRICE: $2,000 BODY: Victoria, leather top SEATS: 3 to 5 persons WEIGHT: 2,500 pounds WHEEL BASE: 80 inches TREAD: 56 inches TIRES, FRONT: 32x2½ in. (solid)	TIRES, REAR: 34x2½ in. (solid) STEERING: Side lever BRAKES: Internal expanding SPRINGS: Special platform FRAME: Armored wood CURRENT SUPPLY: Storage battery	MOTOR-CONTROL: 4 forward and reverse TRANSMISSION: Annular ball bearings SPEED: 18 miles per hour SPEED CONTROL: Side lever DRIVE: Side chain
Baker Inside Driven Coupe Model L.		**Baker Motor Vehicle Co., Cleveland, Ohio**
PRICE: $2,000 BODY: Wood WEIGHT: 1,640 pounds WHEEL BASE: 70 inches TREAD: 55 inches TIRES, FRONT: 30x3½ inches	TIRES, REAR: 30x3½ inches STEERING: Side lever BRAKES: Two foot brakes, external and internal on rear wheels SPRINGS: Semi-elliptic in front; full elliptic in rear	FRAME: Armored wood MOTOR: 2 H.P., 300% overload BATTERY: 24 cells, 9 m.v. CAPACITY: 80 miles per charge SPEEDS: 6 forward and 3 reverse DRIVE: Single chain
Pope-Waverley, Stanhope, Model 53A.		**Pope Motor Car Co., Indianapolis, Ind.**
PRICE: $2,000 BODY: With removable top SEATS: 2 persons WHEEL BASE: 76 inches TREAD: 54 inches TIRES, FRONT: 32x3½ in.	TIRES, REAR: 32x4 in. STEERING: Wheel, worm and gear BRAKES: Two foot and one electric SPRINGS: Long semi-elliptic FRAME: Pressed steel MOTOR: One, special	CURRENT SUPPLY: 30 cells, 11 M. V. exide GEARING: Herringbone type SPEED: 5 to 18 miles per hour DRIVE: Direct
Electric Phaeton, Model 1.		**S. R. Bailey & Co., Amesbury, Mass.**
Maker's illustration not ready—will be published later and of a size suitable for insertion in this space. PRICE: $2,000 BODY: Queen phaeton SEATS: 2 persons WEIGHT: 1,600 pounds WHEEL-BASE: 72 inches TREAD: 54 inches	TIRES, FRONT: 34 x 3 inches TIRES, REAR: 34 x 3 inches STEERING: Wheel BRAKES: Band to motor and rear wheels SPRINGS: Half elliptic	FRAME: Pat. angle and tee steel CURRENT SUPPLY: Storage battery SPEEDS: 4, ahead and back, up to 18 m. p. h. DRIVE: Double chain
Studebaker, Model 13a.		**Studebaker Automobile Co., South Bend, Ind.**
PRICE: $1,650, with top BODY: Stanhope SEATS: 2 persons WEIGHT: 2,250 pounds WHEEL BASE: 72 inches TREAD: 54 inches TIRES, FRONT: 30x3½ inches TIRES, REAR: 30x3½ inches STEERING: By side lever	BRAKES: One operating on motor drum; one operating on rear axle SPRINGS: Front, semi-elliptic, rear, full elliptic FRAME: Tubular MOTOR RATING: 50 volts, 30 amperes BATTERY: 36 cell, 9 plate SPEEDS: 3 to 18 miles per hour	BATTERY ARRANGEMENT: Assembled in three trays MOTOR SUSPENSION: Hung from frame MOTOR-CONTROL: By controller located left side of seat DRIVE: Through medium of chain and sprockets
Pope-Waverley, Model 60B, Surrey.		**Pope Motor Car Co., Indianapolis, Ind.**
PRICE: $1,700, with top BODY: Straight sill, panel seat SEATS: 4 persons WHEEL BASE: 90 inches TREAD: 54 inches	TIRES, FRONT: 30x3½ in. TIRES, REAR: 30x4 in. STEERING: Side lever BRAKES: Two foot and one electric SPRINGS: Full elliptic	MOTORS: Two, special CURRENT SUPPLY: 44 cells of 9 P. V. exide GEARING: Herringbone type SPEED: 5 to 15 m. p. h. DRIVE: Direct
Pope-Waverley, Model 26C, Chelsea.		**Pope Motor Car Co., Indianapolis, Ind.**
PRICE: $1,700 BODY: With removable coupe top WHEEL BASE: 80 inches TREAD: 54 inches	TIRES, FRONT: 30x3 in. TIRES, REAR: 30x4 in. STEERING: Center lever BRAKES: Two foot and one electric SPRINGS: Full elliptic	MOTOR: One, special CURRENT SUPPLY: 30 cells of 11 P. V. exide GEARING: Herringbone type SPEED: 5 to 15 m. p. h. DRIVE: Direct
Cantono Fore Carriage.		**Cantono Electric Fore Carriage Co., New York**
PRICE: $1,750 NOTE: The Cantono Electric Fore Carriage is sold individually at the above price, which includes the attaching of same to any horse-drawn vehicle, converting it to an electric carriage. Complete vehicles are also marketed by this concern. (See page 80.)	STEERING: Electrical and mechanical combination type BRAKES: Electric, on wheels MOTORS: Two; one on each wheel HORSE-POWER: 2½ each	MOTOR SUSPENSION: On axle BATTERY: 44 cells, Exide SPEEDS: 4 forward, 2 reverse DRIVE: Direct, on wheels

Just some of the EVs for sale at the turn of the 19th into the 20th century

Electric Vehicles, What About Them?!?

	Studebaker Automobile Co., South Bend, Ind.
Studebaker, Model 13a. PRICE: $1,650, with top BODY: Stanhope SEATS: 2 persons WEIGHT: 2,350 pounds WHEEL BASE: 73 inches TREAD: 54 inches TIRES, FRONT: 30x3½ inches TIRES, REAR: 30x3½ inches STEERING: By side lever	BRAKES: One operating on motor drum; one operating on rear axle SPRINGS: Front, semi-elliptic; rear, full elliptic FRAME: Tubular MOTOR RATING: 50 volts, 30 amperes BATTERY: 36 cell, 9 plate SPEEDS: 3 to 18 miles per hour	BATTERY ARRANGEMENT: Assembled in three trays MOTOR SUSPENSION: Hung from frame MOTOR-CONTROL: By controller located left side of seat DRIVE: Through medium of chain and sprockets

	Pope Motor Car Co., Indianapolis, Ind.
Pope-Waverley, Model 60B, Surrey. PRICE: $1,700, with top BODY: Straight sill, panel seat SEATS: 4 persons WHEEL BASE: 90 inches TREAD: 54 inches	TIRES, FRONT: 30x3½ in. TIRES, REAR: 30x4 in. STEERING: Side lever BRAKES: Two foot and one electric SPRINGS: Full elliptic	MOTORS: Two, special CURRENT SUPPLY: 42 cells of 9 P.V. exide GEARING: Herringbone type SPEED: 5 to 15 m. p. h. DRIVE: Direct

	Pope Motor Car Co., Indianapolis, Ind.
Pope-Waverley, Model 26C, Chelsea. PRICE: $1,700 BODY: With removable coupe top SEATS: 2 persons WHEEL BASE: 80 inches TREAD: 54 inches	TIRES, FRONT: 30x3 in. TIRES, REAR: 30x4 in. STEERING: Center lever BRAKES: Two foot and one electric SPRINGS: Full elliptic	MOTOR: One, special CURRENT SUPPLY: 30 cells of 11 P.V. exide GEARING: Herringbone type SPEED: 5 to 15 m. p. h. DRIVE: Direct

An Easier to Read Section from the Previous Ad

An early EV charger. Just a bit more complex than today's versions.

A Turn of the Century taxi in New York City. In 1899 90% of NYC taxi cabs were electric. In 1900 only 4,192 cars were sold in the U.S. 1,575 of them were electric!

Electric Vehicles, What About Them?!?

Electric Baker. Note the Appeal to Women in the Ad. The Baker was NOT an Inexpensive Machine!

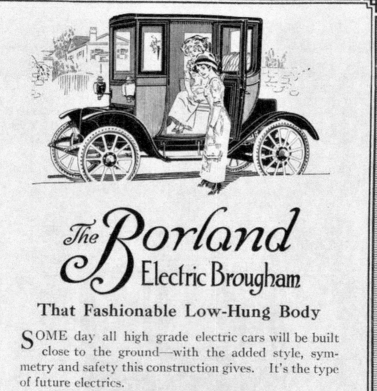

*The Borland was yet Another EV of the Period.
Once Again Take Note of the Ad's Appeal to Women.
$2,200 in 1905 is Around +$65,000 in Today's Money.*

Electric Vehicles, What About Them?!?

Prior to both *ICE* and *EV* use horses were virtually the sole means of propulsion for human transport. The amount of horse urine, droppings and dead animals lying about NYC streets made living in such an urban area truly problematic.

Late 19th Century NYC trolley.

Richard P. Rosenthal

I'm Dubious of the Claim of 100 Miles of Range!

Even Edison and Ford Got into the EV Act!

Electric Vehicles, What About Them?!?

Some Things You Should Know About EVs

This part of the book is to offer up some basic but important information on various aspects of *EV* ownership and operation. Here we will discuss:

- Types of *EVs*
- Their Cost
- Range of Power
- Safety
- Complexity
- Reliability
- Range *EVs* Can Drive with a Full Charge
- Temperature impact on Range
- How to Charge Your Electric Car
  ~The Various Types of Charging Plugs~

Types of *EVs*

This book's purpose is to impart information on *EVs* used for "normal" personal transportation. In other words, cars. While there are a number of most interesting two and three wheeled *EVs* now available, I won't be discussing them here.

As of 2022 there are perhaps a dozen "practical" *EV* models which you can purchase in the United States. Prices will range from around $30,000 dollars (the Chevy Bolt comes to mind) to well over $100,000 dollars. Which *EV* you might want to consider will mostly have to do with to what purpose you intend to put the machine to and the size of your bank account.

If you want a nice commuter car, say for a daily trip to and from work of around 100 miles round trip, then just about any of the available *EVs* out there now should serve you well. Forgive me for being provincial, but I shall limit this discussion to just those models available (or soon to be available) to the North American (most generally Canada, the United States and Mexican) markets. If I listed all the *EVs* now on the international market (most of which cannot be purchased in the United States) the number would be well over a few hundred. I have also omitted (somewhat arbitrarily) any *EV* with a listed range of less than 150 miles on a full charge.

Once again, keep in mind this is a moving target and the list below is only a partial one! We will discuss the realities of *EV* range shortly:

Model	Listed EPA Range in Miles
Audi E-Tron	204
BMW i3	153
Bolt (2022)	259
Bolt EUV (2022)	247
Ford Mach-E	270~305
Ford *F*-150E	250~400?
GMC Hummer	300?
Hyundai Kona Electric	258
Hyundai Ioniq Electric	170
Kia Niro *EV*	239
Nissan Leaf	149~226
Nissan Ariya	250~300
Jaguar I-Pace	234
Lucid	517?
Mercedes EQC	+400
Polestar	233~275
Rivian	410
Tesla S	400~500
Tesla Model X	305~351
Tesla Model 3 (2022)	250~358
Tesla Model Y (2022)	280~330
VW ID.4	310

A word of caution is in order here. While I am confident the majority of models listed above will see the light of day, I have two concerns;

the ranges claimed by their manufacturers and the prices of some of the models listed.

Let's talk prices first. You have noted I showed a range for the Lucid as 517 miles. Wow. Except, that is the company's advertised range of their top-end model. None of their autos have been manufactured in large quantity to-date or are available for general purchase. And as the old adage goes;

> "There's many a slip twixt cup and the lip!"

Then there is the price for the high-end model Lucid with the claimed range of 517 miles; it's an eye watering $170,000 dollars.

The Lucid. Lots of publicity but few being manufactured as of now.

Understand, I am not picking on Lucid. Many of the listed *EVs* above have yet to hit full production, certainly most have not been in the hands of users, and more than a few are advertising both ranges and prices which give me pause.

Let me share this observation with you. Many of the newer, quite beautiful, very exotic *EVs* we are seeing coming out are priced far more dearly than the average person can afford. Until such time as a reasonably priced *EV* is produced for what a "normal" auto costs consumers these days, the *EV* revolution will be delayed.

So, my disclaimer; some number of the listed *EVs* above will not deliver on their claimed mileage ranges, or will be available at a price-point that a mere human can afford, or might never even see the light of day.

Chevy Bolt being charged

Range of *EVs*

There are three "official" measures of range (the distance the vehicle can travel on a full electrical charge using their traction battery) for electric vehicles:

- NEDC (New European Driving Cycle),
- WLTP (Worldwide Harmonized Light Vehicle Test Procedure) and,
- U.S. EPA (Unites States Environmental Protection Agency)

Due to the different testing protocols used by each of the above agencies, significant differences in reported vehicle ranges will be seen by the buying public. Permit me to be blunt; the OEM vehicle manufacturers out there like to make claims as to their *EVs* one-way ranges in the best light possible. Take <u>every</u> range claim made by an *EV* seller with a grain of salt.

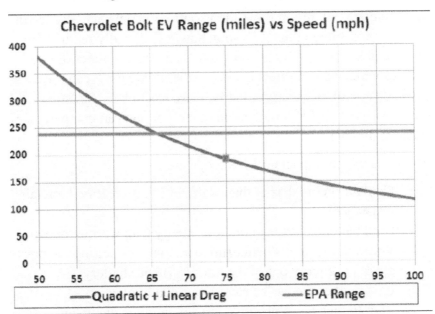

The graph above shows the faster the EV goes the less its range

At any rate, as a practical matter, there is a fourth variation in regard the distance an *EV* can travel, even when at full charge, which should be taken into account. Let us call it;

Reality!

We owned a 2019 Chevrolet Bolt. The range listed for that model is 238 miles. As I'm light on the accelerator (I'll explain in a moment why this is significant) I've routinely seen ranges on my GOM (this is the available range indicator in this model car ~ an acronym euphemistically coined the "*Guess-O-Meter*" for its lack of precise accuracy) showing the Bolt's range to be in excess of 300 miles. If it were winter, we might expect to see a maximum range estimate on the car's GOM (depending on outside temperature) of between 160 to 180 miles of maximum range. No one is lying here or being "cute" when offering up range estimates. These estimates come from the Environmental Protection Agency's (EPA) official testing protocols. This test puts the vehicles through a combination of city/highway driving speeds, within a specific temperature range.

Thus, although you might think the variations people actually see in the ranges possible in their *EVs* somehow reflect badly on the EPA testing, that is not true. It is simply that there are a number of variables which have a direct bearing on how far an *EV* can travel on a given charge of electricity. Clearly, there has to be a yardstick measurement of all *EVs* out there in order that you can compare one vehicle to another.

The factors which impact an *EV*'s range are:

- Cold air (being denser than warm air, thus creating more air resistance)
- Cold batteries (which hold less energy than warmer ones)
- Warm air, which is better (up to a point) for getting the most electrical energy out of the traction (main) battery
- Using either the car's heater or air conditioner
- Rain (which has a negative impact on range due to an increase in rolling resistance)
- Speed! (See the relevant graphic)

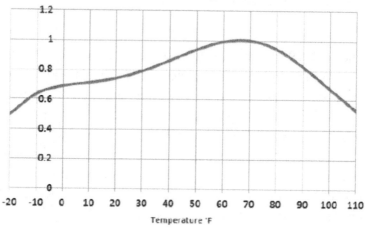

The "sweet spot" for EV range appears to be from 60°f to 80°f

Electric Vehicles, What About Them?!?

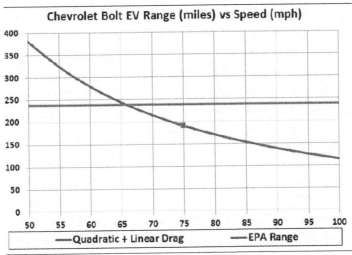

Above is a graph for the Chevrolet Bolt showing the relationship between the *EVs* range and its speed. Once driving faster than 65 miles per hour (mph) range begins to take a hit. Clearly there will be a number of variables, dependent on the vehicle under discussion, as to how significant really fast highway speed will impact how far one can travel in an *EV*.

Below is a graph showing Tesla speed vs range for three models.

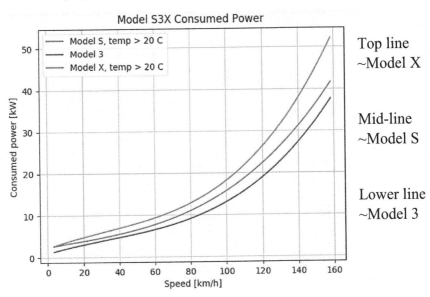

Top line
~Model X

Mid-line
~Model S

Lower line
~Model 3

The best temperatures for maximum range will be somewhere around 70°f (very roughly the best temperature to operate an *EV* is when outside temperatures are in the 60°f to mid-80°f range). As you approach cooler temperatures, especially when you get below the 50°f level, you will begin to see a reduction in the real-world distance you can travel in your *EV*. Approaching the freezing mark, or when colder, will then show you a further drop in range which can be significant.

Is this important? Well, it depends. If you are using the car to commute to work, with a daily round trip of 50 miles, and the cold weather range of your *EV* is 180 miles, temperature will be a non-issue for you. If you have a round trip of 200 miles a day, and when it is freezing out your 240 mile range *EV* can only make 180 miles during the winter, well, that's a concern!

Other Variables

Using the heater, or air conditioner, will have some negative impact on your range. Modern *EVs* are designed to minimize the energy used by either accessory. There are two basic types of cabin temperature controls in service now:

➢ Heat Pumps and Resistive Heating Units

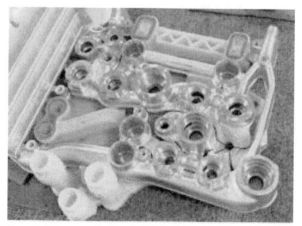

The unique and very efficient Tesla Octovalve

Heat pumps are much more efficient than the resistive type of heater, the latter variety generates heat the same way an electrical coil is turned red-hot for the making of toast or for the generating of heat in a home baseboard heater. Heat pumps not only create heat with less energy required than the resistive type but can cool the car's cabin as well. A significant number of *EV* models are now equipped with heat pumps as they are about 60% more energy efficient than resistive units.

I'd like to discuss how you ought to look at *EV* range claims made by the various manufacturers. The significance in regard miles claimed is very much dependent on how you intend to use the vehicle. Having said that I'd like to offer a rough guide on how to evaluate the auto makers range claims, which I suggest should be practically thought of (most generally) as being approximately 2/3rds of the total asserted mileage reachable by them.

Batteries (the *EV* traction battery under discussion here) are kept healthiest, and have the longest possible lifespan, if their state of charge (SoC) is most often kept between 20% on the low end and 80% on the high end. Understand, you will not destroy the battery if, when traveling long distance, you fully charge up your *EV* to 100% at the start of each day. And the *EV* will not disintegrate if you permit the charge level to creep down to 3% or 4% (some folks do just that when traveling in their *EVs*). But it remains true that to the extent possible, and for maximum battery longevity, you should keep your *EV* traction battery between the levels I have just suggested.

So, if you follow the 20%~80% rule your 300-mile range *EV* has just had its range reduced by 20%. That's brought your car's useful daily range now down to around 240 miles.

OK, it's warm out, or cold out. You, being human, like to be comfortable. On goes the air conditioner or the car's heater. And there goes another 5% of your traction battery's available energy. Let us call it a reduction of 20 miles. You are now seeing 220 on the GOM and haven't even gone anywhere!!

Did I mention it's raining? Well, it is. Another 5% loss in range will be seen (this amount of reduction in range is just a wild guess on my part. Whatever reduction you will see will be due to an increase in rolling resistance, so your speed plays an important part in this equation.). Your *EV* is now down to a one-way range of 210 miles.

Hey, lead-foot, I see you're doing 80 mph. Yeah, I know you want to get to where you're going before the month is out, but keep in mind the faster you go the more rapidly you will deplete the car's traction battery (see the speed/range graph). Your *EV* is now down to about 180 miles of range.

Anyway, this is why I suggest, at least for an *EV* intended for distance traveling, you should not consider a vehicle that has less than an EPA tested range of 300 miles. 400 miles would be better...

Please do keep in mind that which I stated earlier; a Bolt with a rated range of 238 miles shows it can travel over 300 miles under the right set of circumstances. So, when you get down to it, an *EVs* range really comes down to, "it all depends."

	N. America	Japan	EU *and the rest of markets*	China	All Markets *except EU*
AC	J1772 (Type 1)	J1772 (Type 1)	Mennekes (Type 2)	GB/T	
DC	CCS1	CHAdeMO	CCS2	GB/T	Tesla

The assorted charge plugs now in use in the world

Back to the real world. If the locale where you are driving has lots of *DCFC* (direct current fast charging stations) or Superchargers in the area, then much of what I have just written above is only of academic interest. On the other hand, if you find yourself on a dark and lonely road, with a dwindling amount of electrical energy showing in your main battery, there is one thing you can immediately do to lessen your predicament;

SLOW DOWN!!!

Seriously, if you are in trouble because you find yourself fifty miles short of the needed range to get to the next charger, slow down to under 55 mph and you will likely be fine. Just make sure you start your slowdown with enough energy remaining in the traction battery for it to make a difference!

Assorted Level 2 EV "chargers"

How Do I Charge-Up My *EV*?

Yes, we should really discuss this part of *EV* ownership. There are two places most *EV* owners can opt to charge up their vehicles; home and anyplace else! And before we jump into this, let me assure you that plugging your *EV* into a power outlet is about as complex as plugging in your home's vacuum cleaner. But I'm committed to explaining what this subject is all about, so if you're interested please keep reading.

The statistic which I have seen regarding the amount of *EV* charging done at home, versus anyplace else, is +90%. From my own experience in the *EV* world I suspect that is even a bit conservative.

Charging your car at home offers several advantages:

- ➢ It's the least expensive way to routinely put electric energy into your car's battery pack, and,
- ➢ It's hard to beat the convenience of charging up your car's battery while you're asleep!

All of the above assumes that you <u>can</u> plug in your *EV* where you live. This option most frequently requires the user to be residing in a private home, or at a residence with some sort of external electrical outlet conveniently available for their unrestricted use.

There are two main options for the home *EV* charger; 120v (Level 1) electrical outlets or 240v (Level 2) outlets.

Every *EV* that I am aware of comes with an interface for use with one or both of the above sources of home electrical power. These are commonly referred to as the "power cords" or "power cables" or "chargers." Such cables are merely interfaces between your *EV* and the electric grid, nothing more.*

The proper term is EVSE or Electric Vehicle Service Equipment

Charging your EV outside is perfectly safe

Charging speed using the 120v outlet is quite slow, around 3 miles per hour of charge. If your *EV* is simply used as a local runabout, rarely putting more than thirty or forty miles on the car during a normal day's travel, this may well be adequate. We used such an outlet for our Chevy Bolt. Worked out great.

Consider this, if your car is plugged in to a normal wall outlet 16 hours a day, and each hour adds 3 miles of range to your *EV*, then each day you will have no less than 48 miles available for driving. A more realistic way of calculating your auto's actual energy needs is this; if you own an *EV* with a range of 200 miles when at 100% charge,

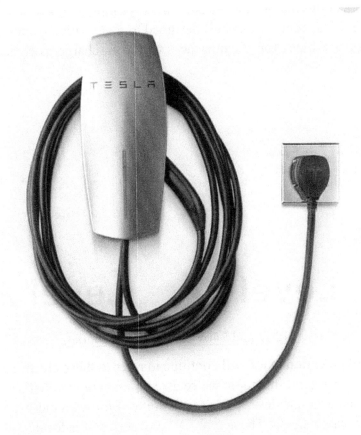

A Tesla wall outlet

and only leave it charged up to 80% unless going on a long trip, then you will have around 160 miles available for daily driving. Thus, every day you get into your *EV*, unless you have traveled over 48 miles the day before, even if using a 120v outlet you will never have less than that 160 miles of range for your driving use!

If your needs are greater than that which a 120v outlet can support, you will have to have a more powerful (larger) electrical outlet installed. The most frequently used type which I have observed installed for home *EV* use is the NEMA 14-50 variety (frequently used for larger electrical appliances such as clothes washers or dryers), which is a 240v power outlet. None the less, numerous other outlet configurations may be successfully employed. All you need is an electrical connector (plug) designed to mate with the appropriate type, one which properly interfaces with your charger cord and the *EV*.

Level 1   Level 2

<u>120v and 240v NEMA 14-50 outlets</u>

I should mention that I will continue to refer to these electric cables as *EV* "chargers," the topic we're discussing here, but that's not really an accurate description (or definition) for what these devices are or what they do. The actual *EV* "charger" unit is located within your vehicle. The box-and-cord (cable) device you attach to your electric car has a technical name; "Electric Vehicle Supply Equipment," or EVSE. The EVSE delivers power from the grid (or other electrical source such as solar panels) to your *EV*'s <u>on-board charger</u> in the first place. Still, most people generally call the EVSE

Electric Vehicles, What About Them?!?

a "charger" or refer to it as the "charger cable" (Tesla uses the term "connector"). So, in this book for the sake of simplicity I shall continue with the custom.

With a 240v electric outlet and depending on the type of charger connection you have purchased, as well as the limitations of your *EV*, you may see from 14 to over 30 miles of range going into your vehicle for each hour of charge. Which means, if you are a person with a long commute, or someone who must from time to time travel significant distances on short notice, such an enhanced speed of battery charge would likely prove to be most useful.

Perhaps you do not have a garage where you can install such an outlet. Note that it is perfectly safe to set up an outdoor electrical outlet for *EV* charging. Just make sure the unit (outlet) used for this purpose is built and installed according to your local codes. I would like to reiterate that it is perfectly safe to charge an *EV* outside, even in the rain! I have done so numerous times and at various locations.

The family's Bolt parked by its outdoor outlet

When using either the 120v or 240v outlets the "plug" connector (the part going into the car's receptacle) which you will likely use (except for Tesla *EVs*) in the United States is referred to as a J1772 type. I will explain a bit more about the various plug types in a moment.

In many ways the Europeans are ahead of those of us living in the United States. For example, in Germany as well as in parts of England the municipal entities there have begun to roll out "SimpleSockets" on a number of neighborhood lamp posts. The driver need only plug in to such an electric power source in order to charge up their *EV*. To take advantage of these new charging stations, electric car drivers simply order a SmartCable from Ubitricity, sign up for an account, and plug their *EV* in.

The Ubitricity charger

The simplicity of the Ubitricity socket allows for municipalities to offer charging stations without having to do invasive infrastructure work such as digging up the sidewalk or installing standalone charging bays. This setup also allows drivers with the SmartCable with its built-in meter to plug in anywhere there is a lamp post socket. An added benefit for both *EV* users as well as the towns that install the ports is the money gained by this generation of revenue for the municipality.

I find it amusing that such lamp post ~as well as other outdoor charging options, were common in NYC over a century ago, only to fall out of use when *ICE* autos overtook *EVs* in popular usage.

<u>Charging Plugs, What are They? What Types are Out There?</u>

In this country you will find several common styles of *EV* plug connectors:

- J1772
- CCS1
- CHAdeMO
- Tesla

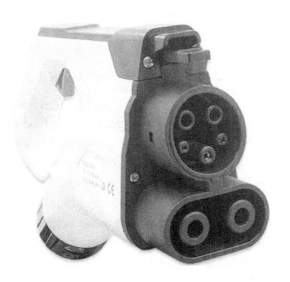

A CCS1 "Level 3" (DCFC) plug

The J1772 is found on all *EVs* sold in the States, with the exception of the Tesla models, which use a proprietary configuration. These plugs are utilized anytime the *EV* owner is charging at either Level 1 (120v) or Level 2 (240v) charging speeds.

A typical J1772 plug, used for both Level 1 & 2 charging

The next most common *EV* charger in the United States, one which is used only for "fast charging" (Direct Current Fast Charging or *DCFC*), is the CCS1 variant. A fast charger site (a *DCFC* station, also colloquially, and wrongly, called a Level 3 charger) may offer from 25kW up to 350kW of power for electric vehicle charging. How much of this power your vehicle can actually utilize is dependent on the model of car and how the vehicle was designed (remember your vehicle controls the amount of electricity which it will accept). As time goes by I'm sure *EVs* will be developed to handle even greater amounts of electrical energy in an attempt to speed up charging their batteries so as to rival how quickly an *ICE* auto may be refueled.

How rapidly the *EV* will permit its internal traction battery to charge up will be impacted by a number of variables, which include, within certain parameters, the power of the *DCFC* station. For example, the

Electric Vehicles, What About Them?!?

Chevrolet Bolt has been designed to take in no more than around 54kW of electrical energy during charging. In general, the Bolt will max out its charge speed when using around a 150kW power unit (commonly found at Electrify America (*EA*) sites as well as at several other *DCFC* stations run by other companies such as EVGo and ChargePoint). I have been informed, and it is my experience, there is no speed advantage in using higher output chargers in the Bolt, such as the 350kW chargers found at *EA* locations. Indeed, I have used *DCFC* chargers with an output of 62.5kW (ChargePoint) and they seemed to charge up the Bolt no less quickly as I'd seen done at the more powerful stations I'd used.

Most modern new *EVs* now are built to take in substantially more

electrical energy than the Bolt is able to, as well as to do so more rapidly than is possible with our old Bolt (a 2019 model!). Things change quickly in the *EV* world.

Therefore, keep in mind the normal charge amount and range added you will see coming into your non-Tesla *EV* will be observed to be, very roughly:

The less common CHAdeMO plug

Level 1   3 to 4 miles per hour of charge
Level 2   20 to 25 miles per hour of charge
"Fast Charger" *DCFC* and Supercharger level
(often, and erroneously, called Level 3~miles per hour of charge will vary with model of *EV*)

Speed of charge is *EV* as well as state-of-charge (SoC) dependent. Some *EVs* may see well over 100 miles of range added for ten minutes of charge time. The speed of charge is thus determined by the model of the *EV* at the charge site, to such an extent that a general miles-per-hour of charge time is just about impossible to accurately generalize.

CHAdeMO users are at a disadvantage in the United States. This is an excellent system, except that it never really "caught on" here. Only a few *EV* manufacturers ever opted to use this type of connector in our country, Nissan and Mitsubishi being the primary ones. The system remains popular in Japan and other Asian nations.

At this time, if you are driving a Nissan Leaf which uses the CHAdeMO connector you will be limited to 50kW *DCFC* charging sites.

The "intake" part for the CHAdeMO plug.
The outlet to the right is for the J1772 plug.

Tesla

This company uses a proprietary shape and design for its plugs. The plug configuration is the same for all three levels of charging in Tesla autos, although their high-power units are referred to as Superchargers, and now offer up to 250kW of charging energy for Tesla vehicles. They may soon bump this up to 350kW.

A modern Tesla auto can put over 100 miles of range in their car's battery in about 15 minutes, using one of their 250kW Supercharger sites. In around 30 minutes the Tesla user may have added over 200 miles of useable range in their car.

Tesla continues to install Superchargers around the nation, a project which they began in 2012. The number of sites they now operate worldwide is approaching +3,500.

The Tesla plug type

This corporate decision on the part of Tesla has proven to be a brilliant one, having made their electric vehicles truly practical distance travel machines before this was true for any other brand of *EV*.

In addition, the Tesla Supercharger system is quite reliable. Most recently they have added *Magic Dock* chargers to their units, permitting both Tesla and *DCFC* cars to charge there. As of this book being published there are only a dozen or so such *Magic Docks* in place.

<u>*DCFC* Charging Sites</u>

Until very recently performing a fast charge on a non-Tesla vehicle, especially away from California or the Northeast, was somewhat problematic in our nation. Within the last year or so (perhaps late 2019 and continuing right up to the present) there has been a tremendous increase in the number of powerful, reliable *DCFC* stations put into service. Indeed, a trip from the west coast all the way to the east coast can now be made (with good planning) using the newly installed equipment. And the numbers of charging stations being built continues to grow dramatically.

The reason for this bursting forth of charging infrastructure is the result of a penalty against VW due to that company's unfortunate "diesel-gate" problem. It had been found that the company had rigged their diesel vehicles so that when tested for pollution emissions the otherwise poor vehicle emission results would be falsified into giving a positive reading. This has resulted in massive fines being levied against the company, with some amount of those fines going to enhance both Europe's and our electrical vehicle fast-charging infrastructure.

Wife about to charge the Model Y

In the United States as well as Canada VW has interfaced with a company, Electrify America (*EA*), having them install hundreds of new *EV* chargers around those two nations (also in Europe). See the Electrify America chart of chargers now available as of this book's publishing for the most up to date sitemap of the system.

https://www.electrifyamerica.com/locate-charger/?search=united%20states

The end result of all this fuss? At this point in time, in regard electrical vehicle travel today such autos are now much more practical for distance driving around most of the United States.

There are other companies building *DCFC* sites as well as Electrify America. EVGo has over 800 stations out now. These tend to be somewhat regional in nature, nonetheless they still greatly enhance *EV* travel possibilities. ChargePoint has many stations in place as

Electric Vehicles, What About Them?!?

well as more planned for the near future. There are several other large players out there all helping to increase the utility of *EV* usage.

PlugShare view of most DCFC locations as of 2020. There will be quite a few more by the time this book is in print!

What You Should Know About Using *DCFC* Stations

In general it's a pretty painless operation, with some variations among the companies offering this service. In short:

- Pull up to a charging station
- Read the directions on the screen (as I mentioned, instructions will vary with each company)
- You will probably be directed to first insert the charge plug into your vehicle
- Either use a credit card, the specific firm's RFID card for that company's chargers (which you will have to sign up for in advance or open the "app" on your smartphone for that brand of charger. They will also need your credit card info.), or from your smart phone (you did already download their app, correct?) in order to interface with the charging station
- If all goes well, after swiping a card, or tapping an RFID card or by using your smart phone or otherwise following the

directions on the app, in a moment the screen on the station will show you are receiving electricity going into your *EV*

On occasion (and this is happening less and less) you may encounter an issue with the chargers. Try this first:

- ➢ Sometimes the newer heavier cabled plugs (they are water cooled, so are pretty bulky) need to be held in place in your car's charge port (this was true with the Bolt) until the plug "connects" with your auto. Try keeping some pressure on the plug until it's clear charging has begun.
- ➢ If there are multiple chargers at the site simply give another plug a try. Most of the time that will resolve the matter.
- ➢ If all else fails, call the help number found on the outside of the charging unit. Frequently the problem can be resolved by the person you are speaking with by them remotely using their software interface with the problem charger. I have found the folks who answer such calls to be easy to deal with and most helpful.

In the future, and I cannot tell you when this will happen, you will simply roll up to a charging station, plug in the charger, and the electricity will flow. The device you have connected with will have automatically read your information when making the initial connection and you will be billed as appropriate for the charging session. This is called "Plug & Charge." This is how Tesla handles the matter. More about that company in a moment.

I'll go into explaining about some suggested apps you'll need to use when searching out *DCFC* charging stations in another chapter in the book.

As I mentioned earlier the Tesla *Magic Dock* system, once in place, will enhance the practicality of *DCFC EV* road travel tremendously.

Tesla

Tesla has their system for charging their autos down pat (but only for their autos. Unless you are driving a Tesla you cannot access that company's proprietary charging system (this may change soon with their *Magic Dock* system). And before you become angry with them keep in mind they put their system in place years before anyone else was interested in becoming involved in the endeavor.

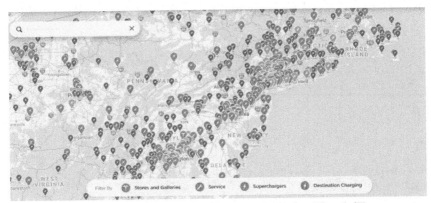

The chargers for Tesla EVs just in the North/East

You simply pull into the Tesla fast-charger station (called a Supercharger), plug in and your car charges. Period. End of story.

Not only that, but in their autos they have sophisticated navigation/information screens which informs the driver of, among other things:

- Where the Superchargers are along the intended route of travel
- How much charge (in time and amount) you will require at each in order to reach the next charger
- How many charge stalls (if any) are in use at the moment

There need be no concern on the part of a Tesla owner when starting out on a long journey. Enter your destination into the in-car navigation screen (you may do so using a voice command) and the computer will do the rest.

Indeed, as of today Tesla autos are some of the quickest to charge *EVs* of those now on the market. The older stations of theirs charge at 72kW ("urban" chargers), while the newest Supercharger stations (V3) have a rate of charge up to 250kW.

I have included a few Tesla, and non-Tesla, navigation maps to show just how sophisticated a charging network is being put together. It is an impressive accomplishment, and if the other *EV* OEMs out there want to stay in the *EV* "game," those requiring *DCFC* stations will

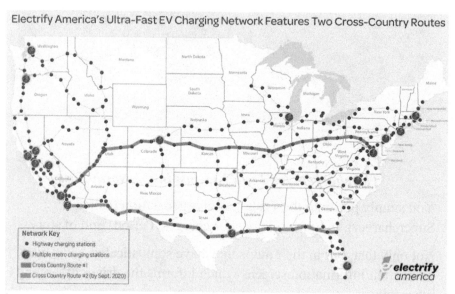

have to play catch-up with Tesla, and really soon.

The above Electrify America map is already out of date!

How to Locate a Non-Tesla Charging Station

There are several ways to handle this task. Google maps as well as Waze will now show you where specific chargers are located when you ask to see one. The best method, prior to making a long trip in your *EV* is to use one of the "apps" designed for this specific purpose. The two I use are *PlugShare* and *A Better Route Planner*. Both are covered in detail in another chapter in the book.

Speed of Charging

OK, so you are not driving a Tesla, now what? Well, you will want to know how much time your *EV* will take when it's being charged up.

My dilemma in discussing how quickly your *EV* will charge is, it depends on, among a number of variables:

- ➢ Power of the *DCFC* station you are using
- ➢ What amount of electrical energy your *EV* is able to take in
- ➢ How much charge is already in your traction battery

While there are *DCFC* stations out there which offer less than 50kW of electrical charge for your *EV*, as a practical matter, and unless you are compelled by circumstances to use a less powerful station, I wouldn't bother employing such a charger during a road trip. They are simply much too slow save for use in an emergency.

A 50kW station, depending on your *EV*, will take about forty-five minutes to go from around 20% battery power to around 80% power. Keep in mind, if you only need 100 miles of range, then a half-hour of charge might well get you to that point. But speed of charge slows down considerably once you have around 65% of your battery filled with electrical energy (the charge "steps-down").

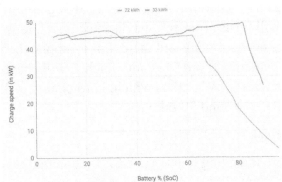

Step-down graph. Note drop off around the 60% charge point.

Insideevs.com

When traveling look for the more powerful *DCFC* stations. Electrify America (*EA*) offers 150kW to 350kW chargers which, for a 50kW limited Bolt, is as rapid a charge as one can get. A number of the newer models of *EV* can use just about as much energy as is available from a given *DCFC* site.

I've included a chart showing charge percent in relation to charge time. Several *YouTube EV* personalities conduct regular tests for such information. They include Tom Moloughney, Kyle Connor, and Bjørn Nyland. See the chapter **Charging Speeds of Various EVs** for more info on them.

Note that it takes about as much time to go from nearly empty to 80% charge as to go from 80% to 100% charge. During a 2,700-mile trip my wife and I took in the Bolt, one day we needed to get up to a 92% charge to make the next station. That had us sitting at the charger for exactly one hour!

Your best tactic, when going on a long-distance ride in an *EV* such as the Bolt, is to plan out how much range you need to get to your next charger destination, add some buffer just for peace of mind, and only charge up to the level required. This will save you time.

Newer *EVs*, with more capable (including larger capacity) traction batteries, will take far less time than older model *EVs* to charge when on a road trip. Therefore the reality is, if you are interested in an *EV* which will be used for routine distance travel, look to the more powerful newer models out there. For example, the very new (and recently available) Ford Mustang Mach-E will charge using the Electrify America 150kW outlets which, Ford claims, will charge the car to 190 miles in around 30 minutes.

Let's Be Practical

Look, if you are intending to use your *EV* for commuting or as a local runabout, then all this chatter about charge speed is academic. Indeed, the discussion in regard the length of time it takes for *DCFC* charge speed is of little interest to you. In point of fact, you will be performing virtually all of your auto's charging at home, while you are in bed! If, on the other hand, it is your intent to use your *EV* for long distance travel on a regular basis then seriously consider either one of the newer models coming out which are capable of taking in a lot of electrical energy in the shortest period of time, or just look at the Tesla offerings. With Tesla vehicles you not only get decent range (±300 miles) but access to their well thought out and robust charging stations.

There is no way around it, you'll have to do a bit of research in order to find the most suitable *EV* which will suit your needs.

A Few Other Considerations

I would just like to briefly touch on *EV*:

- Power
- Safety
- Complexity
- Reliability

Power

If you have never driven an electric auto you are in for a surprise. The motor(s) propelling these cars are directly connected to their wheels. There is (generally) no transmission or drivetrain to suck power from them. Unlike an *ICE* vehicle, which requires the engine to be running within a narrow band of revolutions (revolutions per minute or RPM) in order to achieve maximum power, the *EV* has instant torque (simply stated, the definition of torque is the engine's rotational force. Its "oomph" or pulling power if you will.). You will find that when you press down on the accelerator of an *EV* the car will move forward instantly, and with remarkable speed. Our little Bolt had a 0 to 60 mph time of 6.5 seconds! The Tesla long-range Model Y does that distance in 4.1 seconds. More sporting *EVs* see 0 to 60 mph speeds of under 3 seconds (the Tesla model S Plaid in less than 2 seconds!).

Trust me on this one, *EVs* are powerful capable vehicles.

Safety

Safety how? The Tesla model 3 has come in as the safest car on the road according to the National Highway Traffic Safety Administration. The model 3 achieved a perfect 5-star safety rating in every category and sub-category, and according to that agency was shown to have the lowest probability of occupant injury of all cars that government safety agency has ever tested.

EVs don't have a thin-walled fuel tank holding highly explosive gasoline (one gallon of gasoline is equivalent to 14 sticks of dynamite in explosive force. Which is why some of the most powerful, non-nuclear bombs the military uses, *Fuel-Air Explosives*, use similar hydrocarbon liquids as their main source of destructive energy).

In a nutshell, *EVs* are safe. Oh, and they do not "self-ignite!"

Complexity

I am not sure how to answer this question. How complex is your home computer? Your electric vacuum cleaner? Your home's house fans? An *EV* is some combination of a computer, battery, and motor. The designs are fundamentally simpler than those of *ICE* autos, created by talented teams of engineers, intending on not having their users fret over having to give much thought at all in order to operate them.

Reliability

How reliable is an *EV*? Very. Our Bolt required its first major maintenance at either 150,000 miles or at five years, whichever came first. What needed to be done? I was supposed to have the traction battery cooling and heating liquid flushed out and replaced with fresh.

I don't believe Tesla has any specified schedule for maintenance.

In the real world, for your *EV*, you will replace tires, windshield wiper blades, replenish windshield washer fluid and I think it would be prudent, every five years of so, to flush out your brake fluid and replace it with fresh (something which you should do with any vehicle, *ICE* or *EV*!).

A bank of Electrify America fast chargers

A Few Other Things You Should Know

Battery Temperature Management

There is but a single *EV* now being made that does not offer some temperature control of their main battery pack. This is the Nissan Leaf, an *EV* first produced around 2010. While the Leaf works just fine when operated in a moderate temperature zone, say with summer highs rarely seeing the mid-90*f* range, when driven in warmer climes the battery suffers greatly.

This is unfortunate for a number of reasons. Firstly the Leaf is a very nice automobile and second, Nissan could have "had" the *EV* market had that company come out with a Leaf which had a well thought out battery temperature management (BTM) system.

At any rate when considering the purchase of an *EV*, especially a model for use as a vehicle for distance travel, you ought to pay attention to the system in place for modulating the internal temperature of the traction battery.

Richard P. Rosenthal

One Pedal Driving

This is one of the neatest advantages of operating an *EV*, the ability to forgo the need to use the auto's brakes most of the time. Some people love this ability, others not so much. My wife and I simply would not want to drive a vehicle which does not have this ability. Once you become used to this system you won't want to go back to plan old brakes!

When an *EV* operator removes their foot from the accelerator pedal not only does the vehicle slow down but at the same moment electricity, generated by the electric motor moving in reverse, putting energy back into the battery pack.

The return of energy into the traction battery is called regenerative braking. In most *EVs* the driver can modulate the amount of regenerative braking used in the car. Because of this system the brakes of most *EVs* last a long, long time!

How to Pick the Appropriate *EV*

Permit me to be blunt; if you cannot charge your *EV* either at home or at work then I don't think an *EV* is a suitable auto for your needs.

Fine, so you want to buy an *EV*. We've touched on this before. First thing is you (and only you) know to what purpose your electric vehicle will be put to.

Let's pretend you want to simply "dip your toes" in the world of *EVs*. In other words this vehicle will be used almost solely as a local runabout. No problem, in that case just about any modern *EV* would suite your purpose. Furthermore you will have a pretty broad selection (prices and models) to choose from. Personal preference rules here.

One suggestion I have for you is for you to consider the basic offerings of the various manufacturers. You only wish a vehicle for local use, so range if of no real concern. Anything out there with an EPA range of around 250 miles should be just fine.

Why 250 miles? Because if your battery's chemistry is the "normal" nickel/cobalt type then in order to get maximum life from your new auto you'll want to routinely charge up the new *EV* to no more than 80% SoC.

Which means the actual range would be on the order of 200 miles useable on a daily basis.

Now, if your *EV* uses LFP (lithium iron phosphate) as its chemistry then you may safely charge up your new *EV* to 100% every day. Thus, screwy as this sounds, while a LFP *EV* may have an EPA range of 280 miles or so, such an *EV* with its 280 miles of range, charged to 100% every day, can routinely go further than one with a longer-range *EV* normally reduced by 20%.

LFP batteries have a long life as well, but that is a separate discussion.

OK, you've picked the *EV* you wish to buy. What are you going to do with it when you get it home? In other words how will you keep this new beast charged?

Pretty simple really. Virtually all newly manufactured electric cars come with their own *EVSE* (Its Electrical Vehicle Service Equipment. We've discussed this subject earlier. This is your "charge" cord. Recall that your charger is actually an internal part of your *EV*.)

These "charge" cords come in a few general configurations; some are equipped with plugs for 120v outlets while others are ready for 240v NEMA 14-50 outlets. And some are ready for either type.)

For local use the 120v plug might well suffice (it will give you around four miles of range per charge hour). If you need to travel longer ranges on a routine basis you ought to put in a 240v outlet for your new *EV,* good for around thirty miles of range per charging hour.

***

Richard P. Rosenthal

Distance Travel by EV?~Read This First!!

Fair warning; some of the material in this chapter either has already been discussed in other parts of the book or will come up again.

~

EVs are wonderful driving machines. None the less, you need to ask yourself to what purpose are you going to put your new electric vehicle? If local driving then there are many awesome new cars coming out on a regular basis. On the other hand, at this moment in time there are only a few vehicle manufacturers out there which sell machines that will permit you to travel serious distances, safely, easily, surely and with minimal input on your behalf while in your *EV*.

Tesla is one such manufacturer.

I am unaware of any other *EV* manufacturer which offers the necessary interface and road charging information sufficient to meet the needs of their vehicle's operators.

The ONLY people who can easily and successfully utilize an *EV* for long distance, road-trip type travel, other than those operating Teslas, are the relatively small number of people who are intensely interested in these vehicles, and who are able to manually map out a way to find one charging station after another while on a long-distance journey.

Most people are folks who simply wish to use their autos with a minimum of fuss. That's not a sin. They want to get in their cars, maybe tell Waze or Google maps where they want to go, and just follow their noses, stopping off to fuel/charge up their vehicles as necessary.

Most *EVs* are more complex than that.

Most people want to get into a vehicle, start it up and just go to where they want to go. To travel any distance in an *EV* requires the following:

> ➢ An internal navigation system that will direct the user to whatever vehicle fast charging stations are needed to get to wherever they are headed.

Electric Vehicles, What About Them?!?

- ➤ An automatic battery heating system which heats up the traction battery of the *EV* prior to the next charge, in order to speed the charging process up.

Let me be clear; for commuting and local rides *EVs* are wonderful. Almost any *EV* out there would work out just fine for most people. This chapter is only about traveling long distances in an electric vehicle.

Here's the problem. You get into your new, super-duper, 300-mile range, electric wonder car. You live in *Anywhere USA* and you want to visit mom and dad who live in *Podunk USA*, 787 miles away. Gotta show off the new car to them, right?

Let me start off by suggesting that whatever the EPA rating of range is shown for your new *EV*, figure you're good for around **70%** of that distance with a 100% SoC start while driving at highway speeds. It's not a conspiracy. The EPA shows a blended range of city and highway travel. Most (not all) *EVs* won't get you the full distance shown when you travel at highway speeds. Sorry about that.

Anyway, back to visiting the folks. It'll be an adventure you figure.

It may well be.

The dealer assured you there were plenty of chargers out on the road these days, which is true. So, no worries. But he didn't tell you anything else, such as how to charge the car up, what to do if the charger didn't function properly, even how to locate necessary chargers along your route.

Indeed, most car sales people don't have a clue about such things.

He (or she) just wanted to sell you a car. That's his/her job. The rest is up to you.

So, you get in to a fully charged *EV*. Range is showing 310 miles on the "Guess-O-Meter." This is the "GOM," the indicator on the *EV* showing you your approximate range available at your SoC.

Spoiler alert; it's being optimistic.

Range is a matter of several variables, and not in this exact order:

- ➤ Temperature (colder, battery holds less energy=less range)

- Wind (on the nose=less range)
- Rain/snow (more friction, slows the car down=less range)
- Speed (faster=less range)

I go into the details of why the above are considerations in other parts of the book, so I won't do so here. Just trust me on this one.

So, you punch in your destination into your car's computer/infotainment system. Depending on the model of *EV* various bits of information may pop up. The problem being, except for Tesla *EVs*, the information shown will likely be of limited value unless you actually know what you are doing.

If distance travel with the new *EV* you are considering buying is on your checklist of must-haves then I suggest you do the following; come prepared so that when at the auto dealership you ask the salesperson, "Show me how this car will navigate to (fill in the blank here of the name of a city at least 500 miles distance)." Depending on what you see next will determine whether or not that vehicle should remain on your list of potential *EV* purchases.

Some systems show you every charger in the area. Of all different levels, only of which fast chargers are of any utility on a trip. After all, a Level 2 charger will give you all of around thirty miles of range in an hour of charge. So, a nav map filled with such chargers would be of very limited use.

What exactly are you going to do with that confusing jumble of data?

On the other hand a number of the newer models have useful screens which will help you navigate to your next destination and consider the chargers you ought to stop at along the route. I know that the Ioniq 5 and Rivian series have this ability. I'm certain other *EVs* do as well. You should check before buying.

OK, so you read this book and you've pre-planned your road trip. Congratulations. You know which fast charger stops you want to get to.

Electric Vehicles, What About Them?!?

Off you go. It's a nice day, maybe 50 degrees outside, so you find your range is a bit less than what was originally shown on the GOM (it's cool out) but manageable.

You pull up to the charger. You have the correct app (or card) for that system. You already knew that each system requires a different app, and each system has you interface them "their way." And you have signed up for them all!

You plug the fast charger into your *EV*, open up the app and follow the directions. The gods are with you. The charger station is working, the system recognizes you, and in around two or three minutes the juice flows.

Since you had no way of pre-heating the car's traction battery, instead of the advertised 350kW, or 200kW or 125kW speed of charge you are expecting to receive you see you are getting only around half that amount. A bit disappointing, but you'll live.

The above vignette is a positive view of how a non-Tesla operator might fair during a road trip so long as everything goes smoothly.

Now, if you were in a Tesla, just prior to your trip you would:

- Push in on a button on your steering wheel and loudly state, "Navigate to *Podunk* USA."
- Your Tesla would consider your command for a moment, show you your desired destination on the screen and ask you is this really where you want to go?
- Yup. Touch the screen for "OK."
- A voice will now come up telling you how to get there as well as where you'll be stopping for a charge.

Off you go.

You get to the first Supercharger (that's what Tesla names their fast chargers). You plug in the charger and start charging. Period. No fiddling with anything. That is called "plug and charge." Someday this will be the norm when at any fast-charging station. Just not at this moment in the *EV* world.

Your car's main screen will inform you when you have enough electrical energy to unplug and head off to the next Supercharger as shown on your nav screen.

That's it. Done. Nothing more to do. Really.

One other option Tesla drivers have. You can now procure an adapter, made for Tesla *EVs*, which will permit you to use *EVERY SINGLE DCFC CHARGER* in the nation. Honest.

Tesla now makes these CCS1 adapters available to buyers in this country for $175 dollars. Prior to this the only source was through South Korea, where I purchased our unit.

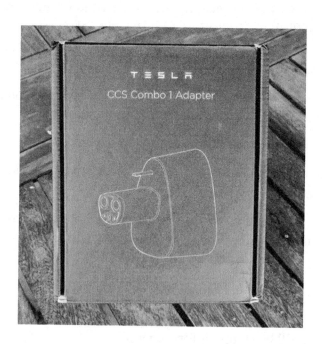

Yes, it really is a Tesla part!

The verbiage below came directly from the Tesla site:

Expand your fast charging options with the Tesla CCS Combo 1 Adapter. The adapter offers charging speeds up to 250kW and can be used at third-party charging networks.

Electric Vehicles, What About Them?!?

The CCS Combo 1 Adapter is compatible with most Tesla vehicles. Some vehicles may require a retrofit to enable use of the CCS Combo 1 Adapter. Sign in to your Tesla account to check compatibility.

Note: For vehicles requiring a retrofit, please check back in early 2023 for availability.

Richard P. Rosenthal

Wife plugging in our Tesla model Y at an Electrify America site, using a CCS1 adapter.

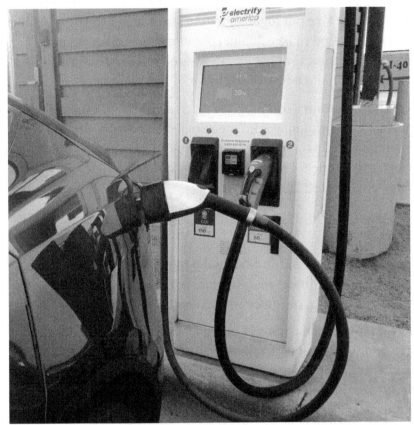

Our Tesla model Y charging at another Electrify America station.

Richard P. Rosenthal

Boring Stuff

"Knowledge is Good"

Fair warning; some of the material in this chapter either has already been discussed in other parts of the book or will come up again. None the less I've put together a number of items which I feel the reader might find to be of value, but which are either boringly "dense" or technical in nature, and which might be skimmed over during the initial reading of the book.

The **kilowatt-hour** (commonly written as **kWh**) is a unit of energy equal to 3600 kilojoules (3.6 megajoules). The kilowatt-hour is commonly used as a billing unit for energy delivered to consumers by electric utilities. This unit of energy is equal to one kilowatt (kW) of power sustained for one hour.*

Distinguishing Between Kilowatt-Hours-kWh (Energy) and Kilowatts-kW (Power)

Energy is the work performed; and power is the *rate of delivery* of energy. Energy is measured in *joules*, or *watt seconds*. Power is measured in *watts*, or *joules per second*.

For example, a battery stores energy. When the battery delivers its energy, it does so at a certain power, that is, the rate of delivery of the energy. The higher the power, the quicker the battery's stored energy is delivered. A higher power output will cause the battery's stored energy to be depleted in a shorter time period.

*(Above material taken from Wikipedia~Kilowatt-hour: https://en.wikipedia.org/wiki/Kilowatt-hour)

**A kilowatt, denoted kW, is a *rate of energy flow*. It is similar to the gallons per minute that a water hose or pump can deliver.

A kilowatt-hour, denoted kWh, is a *quantity of electricity*, similar to a gallon of water. A bigger battery pack with a higher number of kWh will hold more electricity, just as a bigger bucket will hold more gallons of water.

If you plug in your *EV* to a 50kW charging station, and it runs at full power for one hour (this never, in fact, happens), how much energy would it pump into your car's battery? That's right: 50kWh, because 50kW multiplied by 1-hour equals 50kWh.

**(*Electric Vehicle Charging for Dummies*, June 10, 2019 Chris Nelder https://rmi.org/electric-vehicle-charging-for-dummies/)

EV Batteries

Now Let's Talk About Battery Sizes.

The Nissan LEAF for example, is available in two different battery sizes: 40kWh and 62kWh. Suppose you had a 40kWh model, and you bought a 7kW home charging station for it. If you started charging it with a completely empty battery (which you would likely never do, but stay with me) and charged it at maximum energy until it was full, how long would it take to get a full charge? That's correct, about 6 hours (40kWh divided by 7kW equals 5.7 hours).

Now how long would it take (only in theory) if you did the same thing, only you did it using a 50kW fast charger? Right again, under an hour (40kWh divided by 50kW equals 0.8 hours, or 48 minutes).

EV Range

Now that you know how to understand charging stations and cars, the only thing left to learn is to see how all this stuff impacts your *EV's* range.

If you had a Tesla Model X, it might go around 2.5 miles on a kilowatt-hour of energy (kWh). Suppose you had one with a 100kWh battery pack. How far could it go on a charge, in theory, if you could use the entire battery? Again, you probably couldn't, and wouldn't, thanks to certain details I won't bore you with now, but just bear with me on this. 100kWh multiplied by 2.5 miles per kWh equals 250 miles.

Now let's take the Nissan LEAF with the 40kWh battery pack again. If you drive it very efficiently under favorable conditions, it can probably go 5 miles per kWh. So, what is its range in theory? 40kWh multiplied by 5 miles per kWh equals 200 miles.

Therefore, the Nissan LEAF with the 40kWh battery pack can go almost as far on a charge as a Tesla Model X, a vehicle with a battery pack that's more than twice as large!

Now, let us try one last test of your new knowledge, and figure out how much range you can get per minute of charging.

Suppose you charged up the Tesla Model X with its 100kWh battery pack at a 150kW fast charger at the maximum rate of charge. How many miles of range could you get per minute of charging? Well, 150 kW multiplied by 1 hour is 150kWh, divided by 60 minutes (an hour of time), equals 2.5 kilowatt-hours delivered per minute of charging. Multiply that by 2.5 miles of range per kilowatt-hour and you get 6.25 miles of range per minute of charging.

Now let us try the same example with the Nissan LEAF. The charger is the same, so you still get 2.5 kilowatt-hours delivered per minute of charging. But the LEAF can go 5 miles on a kilowatt-hour. So 2.5 kWh multiplied by 5 miles per kWh equals 12.5 miles of range per minute of charging—double the distance that the Model X could get for charging the same number of minutes (if the LEAF was designed to accept that amount of energy...)! Intuitively, this makes sense, since the Model X, at 2.5 mi/kWh, gets roughly half the fuel (energy) efficiency of a LEAF, at 5 mi/kWh.

The above examples are all theoretical and not "real world." But now you see why it's nonsensical to explain the power rating of an *EV* charger in terms of miles per minute of charging: It all depends on the vehicle and how much electricity it is designed and able to accept.

***

A Preface to the Next Chapter on new EVs Expected to Come on the Market Soon

I just had to add a bit of additional observation here. The *EV* world is just a tad bit nutty. There are lots of "coming soon," "coming next summer," "planned to arrive summer of 2025/26/27," vehicles out there. And very few will ever see a production line.

I think the *YouTube* personality and *EV* expert Kyle Connor has the best approach to these projected vehicles, as well as concept cars which are also touted by manufacturers. Kyle has no interest in commenting on any of them until they are actually being produced. Period, end of discussion.

Sure, it's fun to look at fusion-powered cars (I jest), flying cars, autonomous cars, *EVs* that will travel 400-miles on a single charge and cost $30,000 dollars, all very entertaining.

And most, if not the vast majority of them will either never see scale production or are the feverish wishes of some entrepreneur seeking funding along with a willing writer anxious to pen another puff-piece about fanciful electric vehicles.

I do not wish to come across as being negative. I'm not. I am sure *EVs* will, at some future date, come to dominate the personal (and commercial) ground transportation market. I simply want to be realistic in reporting to my readers what is out there for them to actually purchase.

Richard P. Rosenthal

Some EVs~Cars and Pickups~ Here Now or On the Horizon

This is a tough chapter to write simply because the *EV* market is such a moving target. A few ground rules are in order here.

I'm not going to write about every *EV*, car or pickup, that is being hyped these days. Too many of them turn into "vaporware" and I'm just trying to supply my readers with useful information.

While I might mention a few vehicles which are either on the market now or which I believe will very likely make it to purchasers I'm going to try and limit this discussion to "reasonably priced" models.

Reasonably priced is an issue we could easily get into a pointless debate over. So, while I might mention a few *EVs* which cost over $100,000 dollars I'm going to attempt to focus on the "mid-range models" of around $40,000 to 50,000 dollars. With our current rate of inflation this is rather difficult to do.

In my opinion the reality of widespread *EV* adoption will depend on the introduction of practical, reliable, readily available vehicles in today's $25,000 dollar price range. They are coming. Europe and Asia have a number out there now (which I won't discuss, as they are not available in the States).

Tesla will, I believe, come up with a $25,000 dollar car, the common name at the moment being the "model 2" (though, not according to Tesla!). The head of Tesla, Elon Musk, has stated he is aiming to produce the "model T" of *EVs*. If he can pull this off then I firmly believe he will accomplish just that.

There are literally a few hundred assorted *EVs* either now on the market or which will soon be out. Most, regrettably, are to be found in Asia or Europe. As with pickup trucks I will limit my overview to those models which will be seen in the United States as well as those having "reasonable" prices. First we will take a look at "pickup trucks." I put the words in quotes as this group of *EVs* is so diverse, and has the potential to appeal to so many different segments of the

Electric Vehicles, What About Them?!?

auto market, I'm not at all sure the appellation of pickup truck is even accurate with some of the vehicles I write about here.

Among the brands which will be seen, are supposed to be coming out, or are now available in America are:

- Audi Q4 E-Tron, E-Tron GT and Q4 Sportback E-Tron
- BMW i4 and BMW iX
- Cadillac Lyriq
- Chevrolet Bolt EV and Bolt EUV and soon, Equinox, Blazer, Silverado
- Ford Mustang Mach-E & F150-E
- Hyundai Ioniq 5 & 6
- Kia EV6
- Lucid Air
- Mazda MX-30
- Mercedes-Benz EQB and Mercedes-Benz EQS
- Nissan Ariya
- Polestar 2
- Porsche Macan and Taycan 4S
- Subaru Solterra
- Tesla models 3, Y, X, and S
- Toyota's bZ4X
- Volkswagen ID.4 and ID.Buzz
- Volvo C40 Recharge and Volvo XC40 Recharge Twin

I'm only going to examine a handful of the above vehicles. There are a number of others which I have not mentioned here!

One last caveat (and this goes for all *EV*s). Many manufacture claims can, at times, be overly "enthusiastic." Some of the above vehicles either will be arriving later than when expected or not at all. I have found it prudent, when a new vehicle or model is introduced to the market, to first wait until a few respected evaluators have had a chance to look over these models as well as give them an honest range test, plus a test of their ability to fast charge, before discussing them. These reviewers include; Tom Moloughney, Kyle Connor, and Bjørn Nyland. It is simply the prudent thing to do.

From the pickup models most likely to hit the market first I'd like to discuss four vehicles, in the approximate order I believe they'll be available:

Rivian R1T

This vehicle has been out as of 2022. It appears to be a well thought out "sport and recreation" pickup designed for non-commercial applications.

Specifications are:

- +$70,000-dollar price (?) for base model
- 300-mile range (+400? as well)
- All-wheel drive with an electric motor at each wheel
- Tow capacity +11,000 pounds
- Payload capacity 1,760 pounds
- Limited warranty covers five years or 60,000 miles

- Powertrain warranty covers eight years or 175,000 miles

Rivian R1T

The reviews garnered by those testing this vehicle have been extremely positive. Based on what I've read this pick-up will be a very popular choice for those who can utilize such a design.

Although classified as a "pick-up" truck the purpose of this machine is really closer to Rivian's name, it being some variation of an Electric Adventure Vehicle or an Electric Adventure Truck. I've heard it referred to as a "life-style" vehicle.

Make no mistake, the R1T is not designed as a work truck. This is a unique, well thought out machine intended to take people just about any place they would want to go, as well as carry any reasonable amount of "stuff" along with them. You can even fit a tent-like structure to the bed of the truck for camping purposes.

Once the R1T has been thoroughly road tested by reputable *EV* evaluators we will have a better idea where this vehicle falls in

relation to other similar *EVs*.

The R1S, an SUV version, is also planned.

Ford *F*-150 Lightning

As with the Rivian R1T and the proposed Tesla Cybertruck this very well thought out electric pickup can serve for many duties; workhorse, suburban runabout, or adventure camping, just to mention a few of the possibilities this design offers users.

Having come out in 2022 one look at the photos and videos of this truck shows it to be a serious piece of machinery albeit a really good looking one. It is large, with significant carrying space and capacity for both holding bulky "things" as well as carrying heavy "stuff."

- Payload up to 2,000 pounds in the rear
- The frunk can hold 400 pounds/14.1 cubic feet of space
- 10,000-pound towing capacity

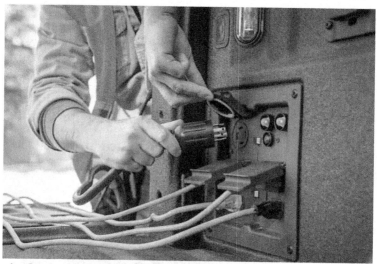

Electric Outlets in the Bed of the Lightning~both 120v and 240v

The Frunk of the F-150 Lightning. It's Pretty Big!

The truck has eleven outlets for power, with four 120v outlets and one 240v outlet located in the bed as well as four 120v outlets in the frunk. That's a considerable amount of flexibility as well as utility.

One other item in regard the frunk; the floor of its very large interior is flat (no lip). Which means you can slide things in and out with minimum fuss. Which is a really good idea.

You can also use this pickup to power your home. If starting from a fully charged Lightning you'd be all set for between three and ten days, depending on the amount of electricity used in the home and the size of that model's battery.

I'm loath to suggest you consider the prices quoted as firm for the three versions. The cost-to-buy range is, as of now, going from $40,000 dollars to around $90,000 dollars. I suspect the initial offerings will be the high-end version. It's simply a matter of economics. Ford has got to recoup some of the cost this complex well designed pickup has run the company.

The *ICE* version of the *F*-150 is America's most popular vehicle. It doesn't take much imagination to see the electric version pushing Ford's current sales leader off its throne.

*

GMC Hummer Pickup and SUV

These vehicles started hitting dealers' showrooms in the Fall of 2021 (they really didn't), with the assorted model variations scheduled to come out through the Spring of 2024. Prices range, as of the summer of 2022, from around $80,000 dollars to around $112,000 dollars.

This is a large vehicle, and the various options; motor power sizes, as well as battery sizes are quite diverse.

The GMC Hummer is a large EV!

As with the Rivian this is less a working pickup and more of a sport pickup. Until the electric Hummer is given a good deal of real-world testing there's not much more one can say about it. This is a specialized machine and only time will tell what audience will be attracted to this offering.

An SUV version of the Hummer is also planned. As with any soon to be released *EV* I look forward to comments made by those able to test the first models when they become available.

Electric Vehicles, What About Them?!?

Tesla Cybertruck

We were supposed to be seeing the first examples of this most unique vehicle become available at the end of 2021. That's what Tesla stated anyway and now it appears the introduction were to be put off until late 2022 (didn't happen...), perhaps even to early (?) 2023. Maybe late 2023...

This is a love-it or hate-it sort of electric pickup. As you can see from the photo it's a futuristic design. I personally like this model for a number of reasons:

This is one tough vehicle! Constructed of stainless steel (no paint!), with robust glass for windows, you could head off to the next major police-action in one of these and be in pretty good shape safety-wise! The Cybertruck has excellent range. And it carries a lot!

The Cybertruck is an exoskeleton design. That means the body, which is of a very strong metal, is part of the structure.

Specifications are:

- $40,000 to $70,000 dollar price range (I'm dubious…)
- 250~500-mile range, model dependent
- Several motor/wheel drive configurations
- Tow capacity +11,000 pounds
- Payload capacity 3,500 pounds

- Towing capacity 7,500~14,000 pounds

Tesla Cybertruck

The Cybertruck is a difficult vehicle to categorize. The high-end version has a reported range of 500 miles, which would make this a most practical distance road-eating machine. It's quite fast at 4.5 seconds to 60 mph. The vehicle is able to carry a serious load, and it

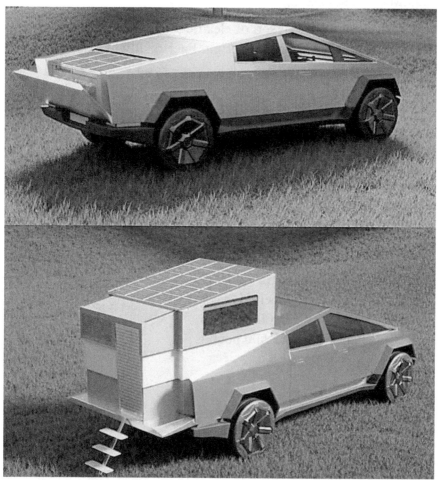

can tow a heavy weight.

Cyberlandr in bed of Cybertruck (a concept at the moment)

Furthermore the design seems to beg for modifiers to stick wonderfully inventive "things" on it. One design out there now is called the Cyberlandr, a camper insert that is completely enclosed when placed in the bed of the Cybertruck. Because of the power outlets located in the rear of the Cybertruck you'd have a mini home on wheels, with all the needed amenities for comfortable camping and "roughing it." There are several other "conception" designs for either towing things or using the vehicle as an RV.

So, is this a work vehicle, a long-range road tripper, a sporting vehicle? Based on what is known now, I suspect this model Tesla can be considered suitable for all of the above

Another "Camper" Concept

One Concept for a Cybertruck Trailer

*

EVs Around $50,000

Tesla holds the lion's share of the *EV* market in the States. Its most popular vehicles are the models 3 and Y, with the Y likely going to reign as one of the bestselling electric cars ever produced. Full disclosure; wife and I drive one.

By this time next year (summer of 2023) Tesla will have several very large factories ("Gigafactories") situated around the globe, turning out their various model cars, pickups, semi-trucks as well as the batteries needed to power them. Between the uniquely well engineered design of their vehicles, Tesla's skill at building very efficient factories, and their very robust large and growing fast charging (Supercharger) infrastructure, this company will be most difficult for other manufacturers to catch-up to.

Tesla Models 3 and Y

These are two similar vehicles, with the model Y being somewhat larger than the earlier model 3. Range for both is in the +300-mile neighborhood, depending on variation desired.

The model 3 range is from around 270 to 350 miles, again depending on variant picked.

Wife charging up our model Y.

It's "Plug and Charge!" Plug it in and walk away.

This is a "sportier" vehicle than the Y, but not by much (the "Y" can really get around!).

Electric Vehicles, What About Them?!?

Just a tad smaller than its bigger brother, picking the "3" over the "Y" would be a matter of personal choice and require an evaluation as to how the vehicle is to be used.

The model Y real-world range goes from around 250-miles to about 300-miles. This is a very comfortable auto for distance travel as I can attest, after having driven one from Arizona to Cape Cod and back to AZ a number of times. Beside handling very well, having a great autopilot which comes with the vehicle, and being able to use the Supercharger network which remains the "gold-standard" for *EV* charging today, the car also holds a lot of gear (mostly luggage in our case).

Tesla Model Y

As may be seem from these two photos the 3 and the Y look very much alike. Furthermore, you'd be hard pressed to differentiate which year any model Tesla was manufactured as that company wisely has not gotten itself into the annual cosmetic changeover cycle which virtually all the other auto manufacturers have locked themselves into. Changes are made as the company sees fit with continued improvements coming along as required and desired.

Tesla Model 3

Both cars look much better when seen in person, and in color!

*

Hyundai Ioniq 5

As this is being written (summer of 2023) this very good looking *EV* is now available in the States. The reviews of this *EV* from both Europe and here have been very positive.

This *EV* has been tested in Europe (Bjørn Nyland did a range and charging test on this model auto. Kyle Connor also reported on this *EV*. See the chapter **Tested Range of Assorted EVs**. The reports have been very positive. According to Bjørn and Kyle this is a comfortable machine for road travel. They reported it charges back up quite rapidly. Indeed, charging up to around 80% SoC took little more than fifteen minutes. *InsideEVs* reported the same speed of charge. See their DC Fast Charging graph below:

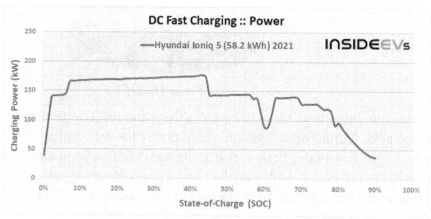

InsideEVs SoC graph for the Ioniq 5

As this *EV* was designed from the ground up as an electric vehicle the wheelbase is quite long (118.1" or over 10' center to center). Make no mistake, this is a full-size SUV.

This vehicle is now available for purchase in the United States but with dealer "mark-ups" so I can only speculate on price. Based on the manufacturer's suggested price my best guess would put the out the door range of this vehicle to be something over $50,000 dollars.

The Ioniq 5 is a beautiful auto.

*

Ford Mustang Mach-E

This *EV* has been out on the market for some time now. The size of this electric car is comparable to the Tesla model Y. Users have reported this is a credible road traveling machine with excellent range (close to 290 miles at 70 mph according to *YouTube* testers).

The Ford Mach-E.

One minor quirk is that once a user has charged their Mach-E up to around 90% of SoC the charge rate drops precipitously (only around 12% or so of kW of energy is allowed to enter the vehicle's battery!). This is a software-controllable issue, and my understanding is that an over the air "fix" is in the works to remedy this situation.

*

<u>Volkswagen ID.4</u>

This VW seems to have been designed so that those coming from *ICE* vehicles would find the interior and operation of this model to be a smooth transition to an electric car.

The price for the three versions hover in the $40,000 dollar range (watch out for dealer mark-ups again!). Real world one-way mileage on a full charge is around 230 miles (claimed range is around 250-miles).

This is one of two VW *EVs* out now, the other is the ID.3, which is only available in Europe.

The VW ID.4

The former head of VW, Herbert Diess, was keenly aware of the competition his company faces in the field of electric vehicles and was determined to offer up a number of innovative machines in the coming years. But he was "pushed-out" of his position recently.

One model which I hope sees production is a version of the VW "bus" named the Buzz. I suspect this very fun *EV* will be a major seller for VW.

The VW Buzz

The prototype interior of the Buzz. Very flexible.

*

There are a number of other very interesting *EVs* out which are available now. Some, such as the Lucid models or the Plaid Tesla model S are quite expensive (±$135,000~$175,000 dollars). Having said that, these are extraordinary vehicles by any standard. Faster than any comparable *ICE* autos, well built, and they offer us all a promise of things to come.

Numerous other *EVs* will soon be available to choose from. Nissan, Toyota, GM and other manufacturers are getting their offerings out into the market. The coming future of electric transportation promises to be an exciting one!

Richard P. Rosenthal

Apps and Maps

*"Other maps are such shapes, with their islands and capes!
But we've got our brave Captain to thank: (So the crew would protest) "that he's bought us the best—
A perfect and absolute blank!"*

From Lewis Carrol's The Hunting of the Snark, a "nonsense" poem, describing the "Bellman's" (the ship's Captain) map representing the sea, but which was a total blank!

If charging stations for *EVs* were as abundant as gasoline filling stations are for today's *ICE* autos this chapter would not be necessary. And in a very few years I suspect no one will need worry about where they will be getting the next bit of electrical energy for their *EV* from. But, for now...

This chapter will discuss, really give out tips and tricks, on how to use two popular *EV* charging applications (apps):

- ➢ *PlugShare*, as well as,
- ➢ *A Better Route Planner* (*ABRP*)

I use them both, and each has their unique strengths and limitations. Both are most useful when planning a trip. When planning a distance drive in an *EV* I urge you take advantage of both. Note, they both undergo frequent changes and upgrades, so please use the information below as a general guide.

In addition we will also briefly look at the Tesla system of Superchargers. This is the most workable fast charging system of any now available for traveling serious distance in an *EV* but is limited to Tesla vehicles due to the proprietary Tesla charging plug and the fact that Superchargers are used (at the moment) solely for Tesla *EVs*. With the very new *Magic Dock* from Tesla (good for both Tesla and CCS1 *EVs*) this may well change soon.

PlugShare

This is a very handy app to use. Once you get the hang of the interface, as an *EV* owner you will find it to be invaluable when

Electric Vehicles, What About Them?!?

moving about the country on long trips. *PlugShare* will tell you, among other things, the location of:

- ➤ Charging stations, from the most basic Level 2 chargers (found at motels, hotels, and restaurants among other places), up to the most powerful units now available (the 350kW *Electrify America* chargers),
- ➤ Where the stations are located along the route *PlugShare* has calculated for you to take, and,
- ➤ The distance between these chargers.

First thing you need do is to download the *PlugShare* app! https://www.*PlugShare*.com/
You should sign up for the app, as this will have *PlugShare* remember your *EV* models as well as your saved trips. Go into either the *Apple App Store* or the *Google Play Store* to do so.

PlugShare view of DCFC and J1772 chargers around Phoenix AZ

Once in *PlugShare*, depending on what has been checked off on the apps menu you may see a "clutter" of tear-drop shaped symbols inundating the map. Their colors indicate:

> ➤ Orange (active or soon to be active, "Coming Soon," *DCFC* fast chargers) and/or Superchargers,
> ➤ Green symbols ("normal" low power Level 2 chargers),
> ➤ Gray ones (fast chargers under repair), or,
> ➤ Purple, a location you wish indicated or marked along your trip for some reason.

Regrettably the sample *PlugShare* map shown here had to be in black and white, which isn't a very good representation of the clarity of the information this app offers users. Just download the app.

In *PlugShare* you can specify whichever charger type you are interested in learning more about. This includes all of the Tesla variations (for Superchargers as well as their destination chargers located at motels and restaurants) and those for *DCFC* charging as well as for Level 2 charging (motels, restaurants, etc.).

Depending on what information you want to see on your map will determine the number and colors of the symbols displayed. If you just want to find a suitable motel for that night's stay you'll only want to see Level 2 chargers displayed. If you need to find the fast chargers along a route you plan on taking then you wouldn't want the map cluttered up with Level 2 chargers but would only want to see the more powerful units. You get the idea.

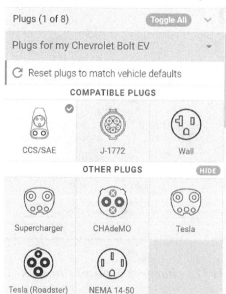

Plug options offered by PlugShare

Electric Vehicles, What About Them?!?

When you click on a charger's symbol on the map a menu will pop-up, filled with information giving the location's name, which company is operating it, where it's located, plug types available, amenities at that site, power of the unit(s), etc. What you will be most interested in is the "*Plug Score*." The score numbers run from a low of "1" (forget about it!) to "10" (signifying the best and most reliable score possible) indicating the practical utility of that charging site.

- Legend
- Filters
- Pay with PlugShare History
- Add Station
- Trip Planner NEW
- Recent Activity
- Settings
- Help
- Submit Feedback
- PlugShare Store

The PlugShare menu

Read the "*Checkins*" for the location. This is where people who have used the station report what they have found at that site. The information they supply is most valuable. In point of fact, what is written by fellow *EV* users should be your primary guide as to whether or not that station is worth stopping at! And I urge you to submit your observations in *Checkins* to the *PlugShare* app for the stations you utilize as well.

PlugShare Main Menu Options

Legend

Click on the *Legend* and take a look at the various symbols so as to familiarize yourself with their colors and meanings.

Filters

This is a biggie. We should take a look at most of what is offered here:

Plugs

If you have specified a particular *EV* then only those plugs useable in that vehicle will be shown by default. However, I've opted to display all the possible plug options out there.

A Bolt can use the CSS1 configuration (used only for *DCFC*), also Level 2 J1772 plugs or, of course, a "charge cord" J1772 plugged into a "normal" (120v) wall electrical outlet. Also displayed are Tesla Supercharger and "normal" Tesla charge plugs, the CHAdeMO type plug (used mostly by Nissan, now pretty much no longer in use in the United States), the Tesla Roadster type plug (a rare bird, don't worry about it) and the NEMA 14-50 electrical socket, commonly used for home electrical appliances (washer/dryer type use) as well as for *EV* charging (commonly 240v/+40 Amps seen in Level 2 systems). Take a minute to review the options, it's a bit confusing at first.

Minimum Power

This is an important choice you will have to make. It is likely, during your search for charge sites, you'll move the slider from 0kW Level on through 50kW, 70kW and perhaps (depending on the *EV* you're driving) all the way to the 120kW option.

We need to chat about the **Minimum Power** option for a moment. The order they are listed is why you might want to see what plugs are out there for each specific power level. Remember, each setting is showing the **Minimum Power** at that site!

0kW: This setting will show ALL charging sites, so it may well clutter up your map with green tear-drops! You should use it judiciously, mostly for J1772/Destination Charger use. When you travel you will find it to your advantage to seek out motels/hotels which offer overnight Level 2 charging, thus the 0kW power level symbols are useful. This will give you the option of having a full charge at the start of your trip in the morning. In order to find such locations you will need to select the 0kW power setting and specify either the J1772 plug type or the Tesla variant (Tesla owners can utilize both with the appropriate adaptor). The various Level 2 chargers will come up as green colored symbols.

In order to clearly see where such low power-level chargers are located along your route you will have to select only the J1772 or Tesla destination plug to be shown. These are the plugs used for both Level 1 (normal 120v household current~a very slow charging speed!) as well as Level 2 charging.

I find it most practical to look at the 0kW chargers available when at the end of one of my routes. My goal at that point is to find an overnight stay with *EV* charging available.

50kW: This is the power Level where most older DC Fast Chargers (*DCFC*) begin (not always. Some units are 25kW, some 40kW, and some 62.5kW). Even if your *EV* is limited to around 50kW of charging potential (such as the 2017~202 Chevy Bolts, as well as many other "older" model *EVs,* you can use whatever power charger you find. Keep in mind, it is the car which determines the power it can accept, not the charging station.

Things change fast in the *EV* world! You will want to use the 50kW setting only as "back-up" charging locations when traveling. Why? Because even an *EV* limited to 50kW intake of power will charge faster while hooked up to fast chargers rated greater than 50kW (generally moving up from taking in around 45kW of electricity to up to about 55kW of charge with the more powerful units)!

In other words, if you pull in to an *Electrify America* fast charging station with your Bolt and plug in to a 150kW unit your initial charge rate will likely be somewhere close to 55kW. If you opted to use a 50kW fast charging unit, you might see a rate of charge of 42kW to 44kW of power begin coming into your *EV*.

70kW & 120kW: I have put these two power levels together as I see little difference in the *DCFC* sites shown when I opt for either one.

This is the choice when looking for the most up-to-date charging sites out there and will pull up all the *Electrify America* 150kW and 350kW stations and Tesla 250kW sites.

Networks

You may opt for those networks you wish to access. There are currently nineteen (19) options shown, but in reality, as a practical matter, you'll only be interested in the main players in the (non-Tesla) *EV* charging world, which I rather arbitrarily consider to be; *Electrify America, ChargePoint,* and *EVgo.* As you really cannot create a problem with using the *Toggle All* button, feel free to look for all of the sites out there if you so desire. If you have a Tesla, that option will be open as well, and will have to be checked even if you specify your *EV* is from Tesla. In a Tesla you will also want to click-on the "*Other**" option (bottom left corner in the Network menu). Don't forget to click-on both the "Supercharger," "Tesla" as well as the "J1772" plug options also, as Tesla autos can utilize all three plug types (they can use the J1772 and *DCFC* plug with a Tesla adaptor).

Include

I check-off *Payment Required Locations,* and *Currently In-Use Locations.* I don't see the point in opting for the *Restricted, Coming Soon Locations* or *Residential Locations.*

Amenities

Be a little careful when clicking-on these assorted options. For example, the *Lodging* option is swell, when you have figured out your route and want to see which motels/hotels are offering *EV* charging. But if you click-on this when filling out your travel plans it will eliminate lots of places which aren't sleep-over stops!! Anyway, look at the various options offered and play around with them. None the less, as a rule of thumb I would leave most unchecked unless you have a reason to look for that specific amenity.

Electric Vehicles, What About Them?!?

Minimum Plug Score

This gives you the option to eliminate sites which have too low a user rating. I suggest you will be better off leaving the score at "0" as this will not eliminate any site from consideration. I have found that not infrequently a site will have a low rating which is rapidly coming up due to timely repairs being done to it. When in doubt about the use of a site read the "user" comments.

Trip Planner

I've skipped over a few of the options offered, which I consider to be of limited utility, and moved down to the *Trip Planner*. Check them all out anyway and play around with them, you can't do anything "wrong" in the app.

The *Trip Planner* is an especially useful tool offered by *PlugShare*. If you are signed up for *PlugShare*, your trips will be stored there. I've made up an imaginary trip to demonstrate how to use this part of the app:

Click-on *Plan a New Trip*. I have for absolutely no reason and completely arbitrarily begun this trip at 4500 Fremont Ave in Tucson Arizona (I don't have a clue what building is located at that location!). The end of my imaginary ride is at a Walmart in Breaux Bridge, Louisiana.

This opens up the *Trip Planner* menu. Total distance there is shown to be 1,290 miles.

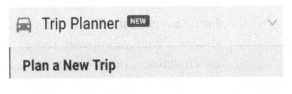

I set my options for the CSS1 plug only (for *DCFC*), with a power rating of no less than 70kW. I want to use the powerful *Electrify America* charging stations to make the trip go as quickly as possible. If needed I could always click-on the 50kW power level in order to see if there are less powerful stations along the way for me to stop at should the need arise. Indeed, the 70kW option will also show sites at a power level of

62.5kW (ChargePoint units for example), which I have found to charge as quickly in the Bolt as the most powerful *Electrify America* sites I've used.

Well, that trip's total distance is too long for a Bolt, so I have to add not only enroute charging but at least one overnight stop as well. Here is the "quick and dirty" route I planned:

Tucson> Chevron Lordsburg> Walmart El Paso TX> Day's Inn Van Horn TX

Overnight stay at the Day's Inn (which is near an *Electrify America* charger), then,

To Walmart Fort Stockton TX> Econo Lodge Junction TX> Walmart San Antonio TX> Snappy's Market Columbus TX> Walgreens Baytown TX> Walmart Sulphur LA> Walmart Breaux Bridge, LA

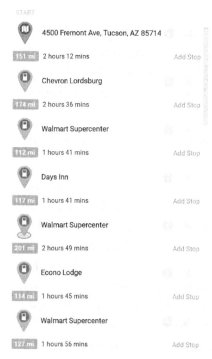

A few comments. The longest single leg of this imaginary route is 201-miles (Walmart in Fort Stockton to the Econo Lodge in Junction TX). Depending on the *EV* you are in you'd best be careful driving such a distance. It is doable in most newer *EVs*, and if you keep your speed down you ought to be OK for older models. For the record there is an *Electrify America* charger between those two locations, but it is not active at the moment (maybe next week??). My personal comfort level is around the 150-mile distance mark between chargers, at least it was when driving the Bolt. Now, if

Electric Vehicles, What About Them?!?

you were driving an *EV* with a legitimate +300-mile one-way range, this discussion would be academic.

You probably noted lots of Walmart (referred to as "Supercenters") locations. That is because *Electrify America* has entered into an agreement with Walmart for the use of their locations as *DCFC* stations. We have found them to be very handy spots to charge at.

Some Additional Notes:

Back to using *PlugShare*. Please save your work frequently. There is a small blue colored *Save* option just below the last stop showing for your trip in the *Trip Planner* menu.

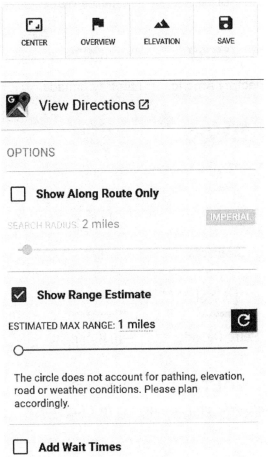

If you click-on *View Directions* you'll be taken to a Google map of the trip.

The next options may be set as you wish. I leave them unchecked.

➤ If you click-on *Show Along Route Only* and put in a mileage figure you will be limiting the chargers shown to just those along your route by the distance you indicate.

➤ *Show Range Estimate* will create a translucent green circle (your *EVs* "range") around part of your route. I don't find this to be of any particular use.

➤ As in the main

menu, and found below the plug options there, is a *Minimum Power* option at the bottom of your trip menu. Set it as you wish.

There are a few other options shown at the bottom of the *Trip Planner* menu. Click-on them and experiment to see if they are of value to you.

Some of the charging networks you can access in PlugShare

***

Electric Vehicles, What About Them?!?

A Better Route Planner

A Better Route Planner (*ABRP*) is a popular *EV* travel planning program. There are two versions that I am aware of; the "classic" one and a newer iteration. Both seem to work well. I'll be mostly discussing the older style here but use them interchangeably. Below are links to both, so it can be your choice. Be flexible as the app is continually improving:

https://abetterrouteplanner.com/classic/
https://abetterrouteplanner.com/

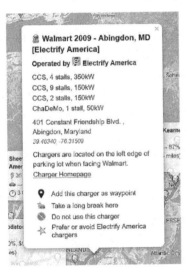

Unlike *PlugShare*, *ABRP* does not inform users of the "*Checkins*" evaluations which other users have experienced for the various sites. When you click-on a charging site a menu of useful information comes up. This includes the number of any chargers which are out of order. (see image to the left)

You will have to fill-in your start and end points in the trip menu. You will also be asked to fill-in the appropriate settings (*Show Settings*) for your *EV*.

Please note the three options on the initial menu; *Show Settings*, *Saved Plans* and *Add Waypoint*.

Show Settings

If you click-on *Show Settings* an additional set of options opens up underneath. Fill this out as best you can. Don't forget the bottom part, which asks which fast chargers you wish to use (the Bolt uses the CCS1 type) as well as if you wish to see Level 2 chargers (not a bad idea, at least when first using the app).

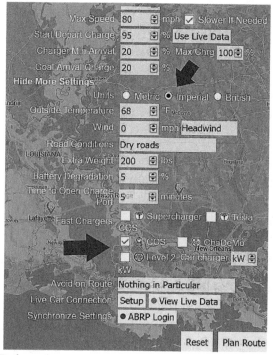

You may then hide the settings and get on with planning your trip. Once again I've come up with an imaginary journey; Rocky Mount, North Carolina to Atlanta, Fulton GA. For the purpose of demonstrating how this app works, I permitted *ABRP* to pick the stops for recharging a Bolt. As you can see from my graphic one of the stops has a distance of 183 miles. That would be a long way to go in a Bolt.

Thus I've added a short stop in Charlotte North Carolina at a Walmart, in order to reduce the distance to the next charger to 125 miles. I did this to stay within my comfort zone. Permit me to comment that some *EV* users, when in familiar territory, will let their vehicle's charge go to 5% or less! Uh, no...

Best route, 12:54	Arrival Charge	Depart Charge	Charge Duration	Charge Cost	Duration	Distance	Arrival Time	Depart Time	Total Duration
Sheetz 504 (Rocky Mount, NC) [Electrify America]	95%	95%	00:00	$1.00	05:12	183 miles		1:37pm	
Walmart 2134 - Charlotte, NC [Electrify America]	23%	61%	00:26	$6.55	02:43	101 miles	6:49pm	7:15pm	
Sam's Club 8278 - Greenville, SC [Electrify America]	20%	82%	00:54	$12.38	03:38	149 miles	9:58pm	10:53pm	
Atlanta, Fulton, Georgia	20%						2:31am		
	4.38 mi/kWh		01:20	$19.93	11:34	434 miles			12:54

My "sample" journey as outlined in ABRP

Saved Plans

Saved Plans brings up any routes you have previously saved. The names given to each are nothing more than a listing of each and every waypoint in the route. The saved routes may appear a bit "kludgy" in appearance, but you can click-on the little pencil image to the right of the name in order to edit what is there and change the long string of names to anything you wish.

Add Waypoint

Putting additional waypoints into your journey is simply a matter of clicking-on the *Add Waypoint* option. You may then enter the address desired (the app auto-fills locations most of the time). By clicking on to the area to the left of the new waypoint (and pressing on the Control key) you may move the location up or down on the list you have made. Experiment a bit to see how to do this. (see image below)

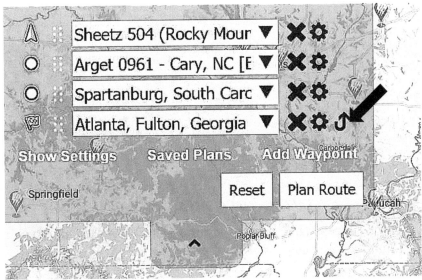

To add a new Waypoint click on "Add Waypoint"

Note the small "hook" to the right of the last waypoint in the list. That will generate a return trip using your installed waypoints.

At the bottom of this menu ("Classic" style) are a number of options; *Reset, Plan Route*. The menu will vary with your version of *ABRP*.

Richard P. Rosenthal

Reset

When you click-on this option this clears all the waypoints you've placed in the route plan above. You can then repopulate them as you wish.

Plan Route

Once you have whatever waypoints you want in your route, this command will calculate the entire trip (as noted above, a little red dot will blink on and off showing you the process is ongoing. Or the symbol whirls. Anyway, it takes a bit of time). On some versions of *ABRP* the symbol for planning the route will simply blink until the task is done. Once the plan is completed you'll be taken to the trip in table format.

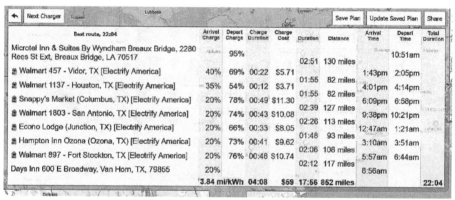

Table format of ABRP trip data

A pretty comprehensive amount of information is presented to you at this time. This includes:

Arrival Charge	Depart Charge	Charge Duration
Charge Cost	Duration (of leg of trip)	Distance
Arrival Time	Depart Time	Total Duration

As you can see from the graphic you may opt to *Save Plan* or *Update Saved Plan*.

The left facing arrow brings you back to your initial route planning menu should you wish to modify the plan in any way.

Electric Vehicles, What About Them?!?

I do wish to remind you that the menus shown here are for the "Classic" version of the app. The newest iteration is somewhat different. Both are excellent. Use whichever one you find suits you best.

*

As a practical matter I have omitted a number of menus you will see when using *ABRP* as well as when you are in *PlugShare*. And once more I ought to mention that my black and white images you see in this book are not as clear or comprehensible as the graphics offered by both of these apps when viewed in color. Therefore I urge you to experiment with both *PlugShare* and *ABRP* before attempting to use either for a first trip.

I find *ABRP* quite useful when traveling by Tesla. Here is a sample route plan below:

Waypoint	Arrival SoC	Depart SoC	Cost	Charge duration	Distance	Drive duration	Arrival	Departure
courtyard marriott shippensburg pa		100%			172 mi	3 h 51 min		08:00
Morgantown, WV [Tesla]	38%	72%	$7	14 min	153 mi	3 h 20 min	11:51	12:05
Charleston, WV [Tesla]	20%	79%	$12	24 min	169 mi	3 h 48 min	15:25	15:50
Lexington, KY [Tesla]	20%	76%	$5	20 min	175 mi	4 h 40 min	19:38	19:58
Fairfield Inn Kodak TN	20%						23:38	
153.2 kWh Ø 235 Wh/mi			$24	58 min	669 mi	15 h 40 min	16 h 38 min	

A Word about *ABRP* premium tier. *ABRP* offers a higher level of service for about $50 dollars a year. Quite a bit of additional information may be had with this service.

Tesla

In 2012 Elon Musk of Tesla decided that the only way *EVs* would become a practical option for general transportation was if their owners could actually travel around the nation in them. So, in a leap-of-faith, he began a program of installing charging stations around the United States, North America, as well as in Europe for Tesla autos. Please keep in mind, at the time Tesla offered the other major auto manufacturers access to this well thought out system. <u>All declined the invitation</u>.

Today there are now many thousands of such places out there for Tesla autos to charge up at. The owner of a Tesla can confidently start off at the West Coast of our nation (or when in western Canada) and easily make the journey to the East Coast, fully confident there will be abundant, reliable, charging stations to be found along their route. I've done just that several times now (15,000 miles worth as of this moment!).

In Tesla *EVs* there is an automatic mapping and route-planning software system which requires nothing more than the owner indicate their desired destination. The installed app then informs them of the places they would need to stop for a charge along the way, how much electrical energy would be remaining in their auto when they got to these stations, and if any *Tesla Destination Chargers* are available at motels/hotels/restaurants along their route of travel.

I have included a number of Tesla charging maps for you to examine. The symbols shown are mainly active charging stations, as well as stations scheduled to be installed at the indicated locations, *Destination Chargers* (Level 2 chargers found at motels and such, handed out for free by Tesla!) and Tesla service stations.

As a practical matter a cross country trip in a Tesla requires virtually no pre-planning on the part of the traveler!

It is a remarkable system and app, one which ought to be emulated by other *EV* manufacturers if they wish to successfully compete in the *EV* road travel market.

The Tesla Navigation Menu

I regret that I must use black and white images here in order to show the Tesla screen options. Their large screen is much easier to read when seen in vibrant color.

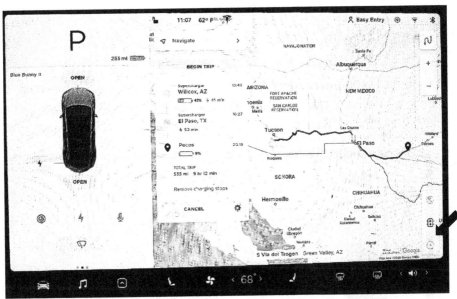

A sample trip from Green Valley AZ to Pecos TX

To navigate with the Tesla system you can either type-in the location you wish to travel to or, more simply, press on the right control wheel "button" (a multi-function switch) on the steering wheel and state your desired destination.

Please take note that the Tesla navigation app informs the user where they ought to be stopping for their charging needs, how much of their battery charge will remain upon their arrival, the approximate times of arrival, trip length and the amount of time the trip will take.

The small round symbol at the lower right-hand corner of the screen (now upper right with new screens), when pressed, will bring up all the nearby chargers available of the various power levels desired. This could be most useful when looking for a motel which has a destination charger in order to permit the user to leave the next morning with a full "tank" of energy!

Travel by *EV* is rapidly evolving. At this moment in time the Tesla system makes distance travel quite simple. I have no doubt that in a very few years, as more and more *EVs* come to the market and their use becomes the norm, there will be a leveling of the playing field in this area.

<u>A Few Other Tesla Menus</u>
<u>(Note: These Menus Change with Upgrades!)</u>

I thought I would include a few other Tesla menus in order to better show what their system is like. Again, the clarity of their menus is far better than as seen printed out in this book.

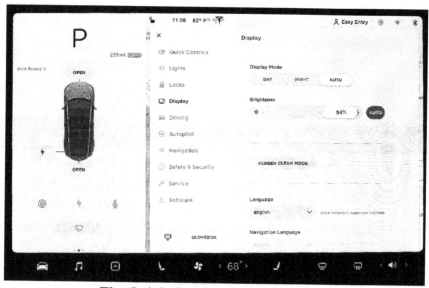

The Quick Controls options screen

The Quick Controls screen (little auto-symbol to the bottom-left) is likely one of the most accessed of those available. Before I explain what some of the options are for, please understand that Tesla permits opening or ordering a wide-ranging number of actions through the use of verbal commands, thereby negating the need to take one's eyes off the road should the driver wish to perform some function or other.

Most of the offerings seen on the screen are self-explanatory. I have also found that the "Auto" option available for many functions has been well thought out and suits our needs just fine.

The "Screen Clean Mode" is just that; when your screen becomes a mess of fingerprints, touch that option and the screen goes blank. It comes alive again with another momentary touch.

"Glovebox" opens the glovebox! Or you can just hit the right scroll button on the steering wheel and simply state "Open Glovebox!"

Another useful menu is for determining when you want to charge the car when at home:

Simply touch "Schedule" and, as seen in the image below, you can cause the Tesla to begin its charging session at any time desired (generally the most cost-effective time as determined by your area's electrical rates).

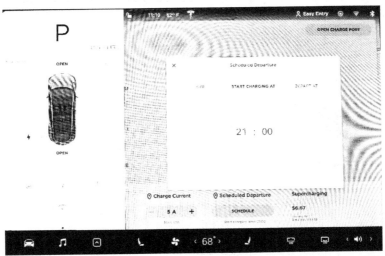

Here I have set our Tesla to start charging at 2100 hours (9PM)

The next image is when the charge was set to stop (DEPART AT). I am confident that once you are in this menu you'll find working the system quite intuitive.

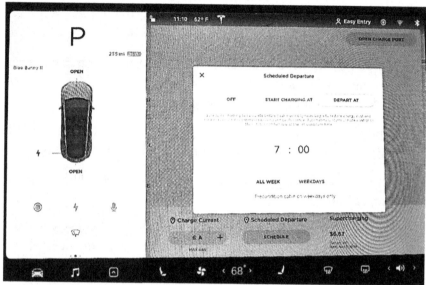

Charging is set to stop ("DEPART AT") at 7AM in the morning.

A few other vehicle control options may be found here

Electric Vehicles, What About Them?!?

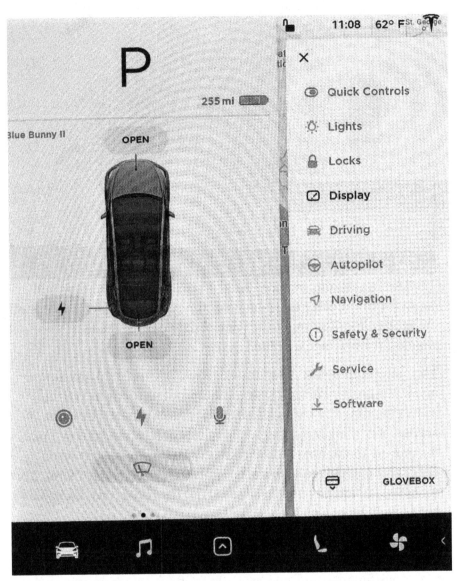

*A Better View of the Options Offered on the Tesla Menu
Each of the Options Above Brings up a Relevant Menu
The Little "^" in a Box Opens up More Menu Options. Recent Over
The Air Updates Have added More Menu Options.*

The Driving options include "Hold" (see arrow above). This will cause the car to come to a complete stop when the driver's foot is off the accelerator. Referred to as "one-pedal driving" this is a wonderful advantage *EVs* hold over *ICE* autos.

The name seen by the other arrow, "Rich," is me (duh), containing my driver profile. When I save various options to my name, this causes the car to fit me as I desire (and this covers a wide range of actions, including but not limited to the seat position, to how I like the mirrors tilted, how I want to see my energy level portrayed, either as a percentage or in miles available, plus lots lots more). My wife has her unique options, saved under her name, thus available to her as well.

I have only mentioned a few of the adjustments a person can put into practice with their Tesla auto. If you are really curious about the numerous functions offered by Tesla for their autos you can easily access this information on their web site. Below is the address for the model Y manual:

https://tesla-info.com/doc/model_y_owners_manual_north_america_en.pdf

Electric Vehicles, What About Them?!?

Magic Dock!!

Tesla has just changed (or at least started to change) the entire *EV* fast charge world with its *Magic Dock*. In short, Tesla has come out with an elegant solution to the fast-charging problem by creating a dual Supercharger/*DCFC* charger.

This system permits the user to either opt for the Tesla or *DCFC* style plugs. Both found in the small black plug-holder seen in the photo to the left.

All the potential non-Tesla user need do is download the Tesla app and they can then seamlessly interface with the reliable Tesla fast charge network.

I am writing this as of April 2023. There are perhaps a dozen or so of the new *Magic Dock* chargers out at this time. Within a year my suspicion is that there will be hundreds, if not thousands of these chargers out "in the wild" for all users to avail themselves of. This will alter the face of *EV* adoption in a way that one can only speculate on.

To the right is a close-up picture of the unit's dual plug container. Once the Tesla app is downloaded all it will take is a few swipes on your smartphone to have electrical energy flowing into your personal non-Tesla *EV*.

On the following page are images of what that app looks like.

First download the Tesla app.

Click on the image at the upper right-hand part of the app. See arrow.

You'll see a number of options. scroll to the right until you come to...

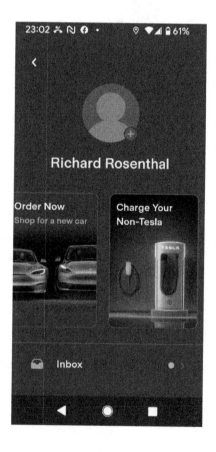

the option to "Charge Your Non-Tesla" and choose it. A map of nearby *Magic Docks* will appear. Hopefully you are already at one!

Pick the appropriate stanchion number, follow the directions (simple) on the app and you will receive power.

My conjecture is, the other *EV* fast charging entities out there are going to be in major competition with this new offering.

Electric Vehicles, What About Them?!?

Electrify America (EA) Charging App

Note: This app, indeed, all the apps seen in this book, are changing *ALL THE TIME*!! ***Fair warning!***

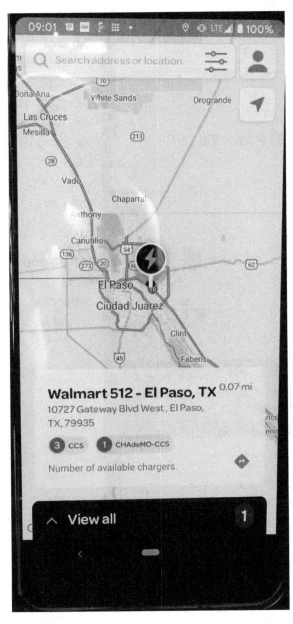

I thought it best, for simplicity's sake, to present my readers with a set of screens they are likely to encounter when utilizing the *EA* app. Please note that the actual screens are in color and thus much easier to read and understand then the black and white images seen here.

This is the screen you will use to locate your *EA* site. Click on the little arrow in the upper right-hand part of the screen to highlight and pinpoint your specific charge site.

As you can see this site is for the Walmart Supercenter in El Paso Texas.

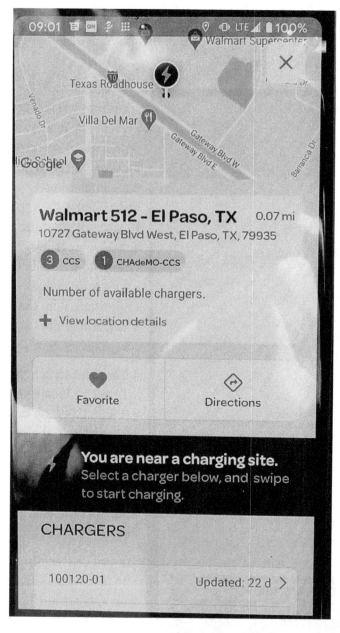

With your finger move the screen so you can read more of the information it contains. You can see that this location has three (3) CCS connectors and one (1) CHAdeMO CCS combination set of connectors available.

You should now locate the charger station you are about to use. You will see the numbers of the stations on top of each stanchion (post). Simply touch the appropriate CCS charger number associated with the one you are using.

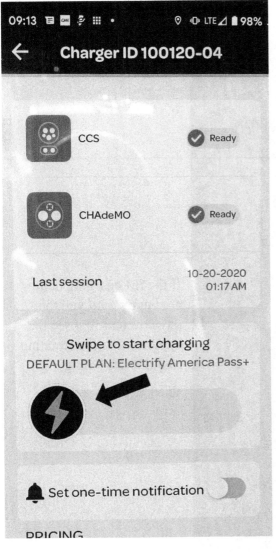

Plug your charger in! (note the instructions on the screen telling you to do just that)

Once you are plugged-in you are ready to activate the charge. The small green "lightning bolt" (note the arrow) must be swiped to the right in order to do so.

While this is going on it might be prudent to <u>hang on to the plug attached to your *EV*</u> (for Bolts anyway) to ensure a good contact is maintained.

Once charging begins you can safely release pressure on the charge plug.

Swipe the green "lightning bolt" (arrow)

If the *EA* charging deities are happy with you this day you will first see the system Initiating (rotating round circle "thingy").

Then, ...

You will be Authorized!

Charging should start in a moment.

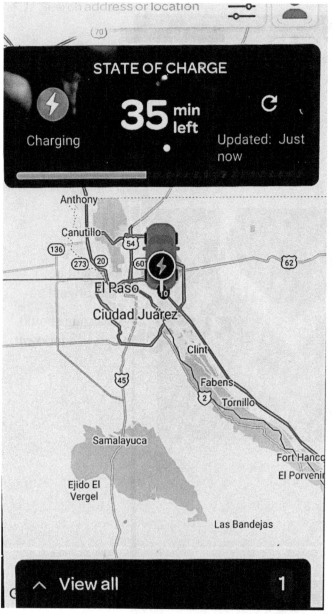

As the charging session progresses, you will be updated as to the number of minutes which remain until completion of your charge session as well as...

Electric Vehicles, What About Them?!?

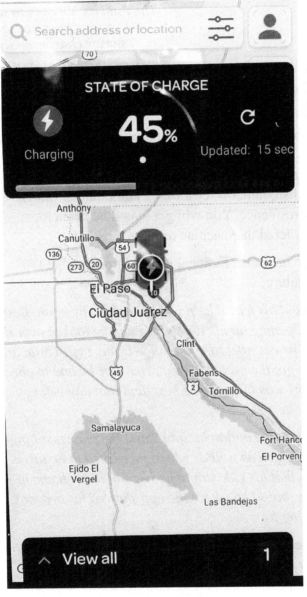

The percent of your current State of Charge.

~

When it all works as it should the *EA* system is actually pretty darn good!

Richard P. Rosenthal

Where Is This All Heading??

> *Whatever will be, will be*
> *The future's not ours to see*
> *Que sera, sera*
> Lyrics *Que Será, Será*

Sometime in the future, and I can't be sure when this will take place, you will need a vehicle to take you someplace. Perhaps shopping, or a physician's office, or just to visit with friends.

As will be your custom you will bring up the appropriate application on your smartphone and speak a few words, stating to the little computer where you are and where you wish to be taken. A few minutes later a smallish, rather boxy looking autonomous vehicle will pull up to your residence. You will get in and be taken to wherever it is you ordered the machine to drive to.

Permit me to engage in a short fictional prediction into what I believe will be our future.

The man had promised his friend he'd be at his place by noon. Best call for a car now. Opening up his Robo-Taxi app he looked over the current choices and prices offered. Ever since Uber, Lyft, Tesla, and the other companies got themselves into a price war he had to check to see which company was offering the best deal that day before ordering up a ride.

Finding the least expensive option he spoke into the phone, stating both where he was located as well as where he wished to be taken. He noted on the app that his ride would be in front of his home in two or three minutes, based on where the app showed his ordered Robo-Taxi was coming from.

Because he was a well-paid professional his personal car was sitting only a few feet away in his home's garage. Problem was, the last time the family used it was three months ago, to visit mom and dad who lived two cities over. He recalled that when a child it seemed that there was a car for every driver living in their home back then. Which simply makes no economic sense anymore. Indeed, there was little point in owning the one car they did have, as all they would

Electric Vehicles, What About Them?!?

have had to do for a longish trip was to order up a suitably sized auto from one of the many Robo-Taxi companies. That vehicle would have shown up at their home and taken them to visit the folks, for less cost than insuring, maintaining or even operating the one vehicle they now had.

Clearly there would have to be another family discussion regarding the wisdom of actually keeping a car these days. He smiled when he considered how much dead space that useless hulk of theirs takes up sitting in the garage, space that was begging to be turned into a "man-cave."

He noted that a small boxy Robo-Taxi had just pulled up to the front of his home. Thinking back to his youth he chuckled as to how sleek most cars used to be, not this rectangular shaped four-seater he was about to get in.

*

The above fantasy scene is highly likely one which will be a common occurrence in a decade or so. Robo-Taxis will be ubiquitous, cheap and the most common form of individual transport used by most citizens. Certainly there will be exceptions. Locations and demographics vary as do the requirements of citizens for getting from one place to another.

In any case those using Robo-Taxis will be driven around in electrically powered autonomous vehicles. Such autos will be available at any hour of the day or night, will drive on airless tires so that there is no danger of a flat which might otherwise delay the trip, and will be far less expensive to own than a personal car, with no reduction in convenience. Indeed, without the need to find inner-city parking the use of such a conveyance would prove to be basically stress free.

As stated earlier in this book the adoption of electric vehicles will have little to do with altruistic concerns over the health and well-being of our world and everything to do with the amount of money people will have at the end of the month remaining in their pockets.

An "Airless Tire"

Human nature, and economic considerations, will control our actions. Fortunately, in this instance, such a change in behavior will benefit us all.

Electric Vehicles, What About Them?!?

How to Road-Trip in an EV!

I'd like to mention that some of the material in this chapter will be a rehashing of similar information found in other parts of this book. Hopefully this chapter will offer a bit more nuance in regard this topic. Here I'm simply trying to focus on one specific skill-set necessary for successfully moving about the country in your *EV*, so will, out of necessity, be going over "stuff" already discussed in other parts of the book.

A couple of tips first, a few of which are pretty generic for traveling long distances whether in an *ICE* vehicle or an *EV*:

> ➢ To the extent practical avoid driving into cities for charging purposes unless that's your actual destination. On a recent trip we took (AZ to Cape Cod) I opted to charge up our Tesla at an indicated charger located on the nav screen located in a major city. Big mistake. Too much traffic, too much road congestion, too difficult even to access the Supercharger. Fortunately we had enough "juice" to continue the trip for another fifty miles to the next charging station. Dumb move on my part.

GO AROUND CITIES!!

> ➢ Try not to head for a charger situated **NEAR** a city, even if it means stopping a bit sooner than really needed. Cities are where there are lots of people, so there is every possibility that even if you find a suitable charger it may well be crowded! Don't ask me how I know.

> ➢ When stopping for the night try, to the extent practical, to spend the night on the side of the city where you will be heading <u>*away*</u> from daytime commuter traffic in the morning. Duh.

> ➢ If practical, try to spend the night in a motel which has an *EV* charger available for your use.

I've mentioned this before in the book, a recommendation offered by Kyle Connor *(Out of Spec Motoring* and *Out of Spec Reviews* are but two of his many sites), someone who has probably traveled more road miles by *EV* than just about anyone else in the nation. And that's not hyperbole. Kyle owns a number of *EV*s and his personal Tesla model 3 has well over 100,000 miles on the odometer. He has routinely crisscrossed the nation in an assortment of electric vehicles (Tesla and *DCFC* types).

To paraphrase Kyle's advice; when making stops at fast charger sites only put in enough energy (generally around 50% State of Charge/"SoC" is his recommendation) to safely (just) get to the next fast charger site. He contends that this will ensure the most rapid travel possible in an *EV*. I've heard him use the term "charger hopping" for this technique.

His logic is based on both his empirical experience as well as the fact that once an *EV* is charged much past 60% SoC (and this will vary greatly from one model *EV* to another) then the charge speed slows down and if you are putting in more electrical energy than is necessary to get to the next location you are simply wasting time.

Full disclosure here; my wife and I prefer to keep our "floor" of SoC level to around 20% and are comfortable charging up to around 70% SoC at each stop. But then, we're in no great hurry.

Here is the reality of *EV* fast charging; it takes as much time to charge an *EV* from 0% to 80% SoC as to charge the car from 80% SoC to 100% SoC. This is just the nature of the beast.

The rate *EVs* charge (ability to take in electric power) varies from auto to auto. This chapter is interested in explaining how to best use the fast-charging infrastructure now available for that purpose as well as the amount of time a "normal" charge will likely take.

Two types of fast chargers are available, *DCFC* and the Tesla Supercharger system. We will eventually examine both but first one bit of advice.

Electric Vehicles, What About Them?!?

A Few Important Points First

I really don't wish to sound like a Tesla commercial, but on the other hand I must be honest with my readers. There are three main capabilities a serious road-tripping *EV* should possess:

- ➤ An in-car navigation screen which will easily, conveniently, and straightforwardly take you to your next fast charger
- ➤ Automatic pre-heating of your motive battery prior to fast charging (this speeds charging up your *EV* significantly!)
- ➤ Plug & Charge charging (plug the car in and your involvement with the charging process at that site is done)

Some cars have one or two of the above abilities. Many have none.

Only Tesla *EVs*, as far as I know, have all three.

An in-car nav system is vital for a comfortable road-trip in order to painlessly take you to your fast chargers when enroute to your final destination. It is incompressible to me that only a few of the available *EVs* out there have some ability to take you to an appropriately powerful fast charger (as well as prepare your car's battery for the charge). Most models require you to manually input the chargers you wish to utilize. That is, you have to insert them into your car's infotainment/map system by hand! That's idiotic in my humble opinion.

Pre-heating the motive battery is vital to getting a truly fast charge, especially during cool/cold weather periods. Your main battery should ideally be at around $100f$ for the speediest input of electrical energy. Tesla does this automatically as you head to your next fast charger (Supercharger). There may be one or two other *EVs* out there with this capability, in all candor I'm not sure. With so many new models coming out it is incumbent upon you to research this matter carefully prior to your making a purchase.

Finally, there are only a few *EV* models which now offer the ability to Plug & Charge. That is, to pull up to your fast charger, plug the unit in, and the charger then automatically recognizes your vehicle, how payment will be made, and starts charging up your *EV* without further input from you. Again, with today's technologies there is no excuse for this basic operation to be missing from newly manufactured *EV*s. Truly inexcusable.

Tesla Superchargers

As of now the Tesla fast charging system, the Supercharger infrastructure, is the gold standard for *EV* fast charging. Not only are these sites quite reliable but there are plenty of them out there, permitting easy long-distance travel. Furthermore, the Tesla main screen (for all models of Tesla vehicles) will direct the driver not only to the next appropriate Supercharger but, as just mentioned, will also pre-condition (heat up) the car's battery so it may more quickly take in the next charge.

DCFC System

This is a bit more complex. Some of the newer *EVs* either now have, or will soon have, onboard maps which will both direct their users to the next fast charger as well as pre-condition their batteries. Such interfaces are, for non-Tesla *EVs* at the moment, in their infancy. Every model *EV* will be different, so it is up to you to determine if the *EV* you are operating or are about to purchase has such a user-friendly system. Be skeptical of representations made by car salespeople.

Road-Tripping in a Tesla

There are a number of advantages for distance travel in the Tesla model of *EVs*. These include:

- ➢ A superb fast charging infrastructure in their Supercharger system (been around since 2012)
- ➢ A very competent navigation screen, which:
  - ◆ Shows you your next SC needed to complete the trip, and,
  - ◆ Pre-heats the battery pack to enhance charge speed
- ➢ Has an adapter available now so that CCS1 type plugs can be used in the Tesla.
  This last asset simply means that with that adapter a Tesla owner can access **Every Single One** of the North American fast chargers out there! I discuss this adapter in the chapter on our June 2022 Arizona to Cape Cod trip.

We'll look at the above attributes to the Tesla system one at a time.

The Tesla Supercharger system is very large, well-spaced out and is growing rapidly, world-wide in fact. There are, as this edition to the book is being written, over 1,770 Supercharger locations in the United States and something around 4,700 of them world-wide. The system is also quite reliable. Here is a *PlugShare* map of the SCs to be had in the northeast. The west coast is quite dense with them as well.

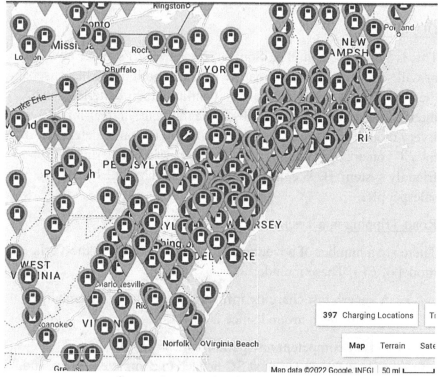

Superchargers in the North/East

Wife and I just completed our fourth trip (back and forth from AZ to MA, +2,800 miles) in our Tesla model Y, using this system. We had no issues.

A couple of hints. We attempted to start each day of the trip with a 100% SoC by staying at motels that had *EV* chargers for their guests. How do you know which motels offer this amenity? Download

Electric Vehicles, What About Them?!?

PlugShare (find the chapter about this app in the book for contact info. The app is free.) and in *PlugShare* specify you are interested in low level chargers (so-called Level 2 type) for both Tesla and J1772 plugs. The symbol color in the *PlugShare* app for such chargers is green. The Tesla can use either the Tesla plugs or J1772 plugs with an adapter supplied with their vehicles. Make sure you set the **Minimum Power** level to "0" (the levels are set to 0, 50, 70, 120 and 200 kW) or these low power sites won't show up.

As I've written a good deal of info about this program in the earlier chapter titled *Apps and Maps* I will try and avoid going into much more detail on how to work with it here.

Below is a *PlugShare* map showing only Level 2 motel chargers (mostly, as I've noted a bit of "extra" chargers shown as well when I've clicked on the **Hotel/Lodging** option either in the **Plan a New Trip** menu or if you've checked the same option within the **Temporary Filters** menu.

Here's what such a map will look like in *PlugShare*:

Map of Motel Chargers AZ MA (symbols are green in PlugShare)

One word of caution; this shows the motels as being deceptively close together. That's because the 2,800 mile trip seen above had to be compressed in order to get them all in. In many cases you will have to actively work the app in order to locate suitable motels having chargers for you to stop at. Consider this to be "fair warning." See an example in the next image.

This map below shows eleven Level 2 sites. Seven are not associated with any motel (rather they are part of car dealerships, restaurants, etc.)! No idea why they are included in the mix.

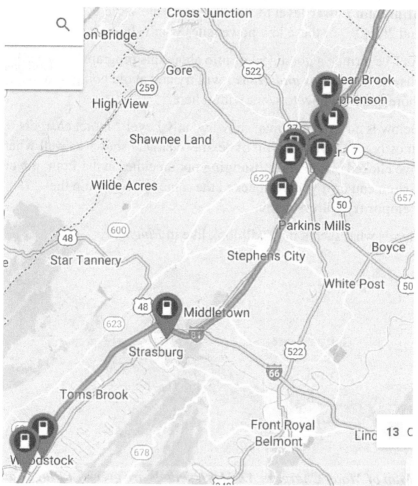

AZ MA Motels Expanded View (PlugShare)

During travels in our *EVs* I have noted, with some chagrin, how many people travel in these machines who have virtually no idea how to efficiently operate their electric autos. Hopefully, one day, people can be as blasé about driving an *EV* as they are now operating their *ICE* autos. The fact that you have taken the time to read this book is a good indication you won't fall prey to the assorted (minor) pitfalls of *EV* ownership and travel.

Richard P. Rosenthal

Places to Go for More Information

There are a number of *YouTube* sites which offer very useful information for those interested in what's happening in the *EV* world. I have listed a few below and apologize if I have inadvertently omitted some useful sites.

Several of those producing *YouTube* videos perform rigorous testing of individual model *EVs* actual ranges. By this I mean the testers charge up the vehicles to 100% and drive them to zero SoC! This is not to denigrate the EPA tests done on such autos. In point of fact it is imperative there be a baseline of data so vehicles may be easily compared. What these testers on *YouTube* do is operate the assorted *EVs* on "real" roads, at "real" speeds (mostly around 70 mph), with the climate controls on, sometimes with a passenger, sometimes driving alone. In other words, just as the owner of an *EV* might do. To my mind, this makes their contributions most valuable.

Among the most prolific testers out there are (in no particular order) Kyle Connor, Tom Moloughney, and Bjørn Nyland.

Under each of the named sites below I offer a sample video (which I picked out arbitrarily and at random).

I have learned a good deal while watching the *YouTubers* shown here and suggest you might find their material of value; especially should you be considering the purchase of an *EV*.

So, in random order:

State of Charge and *InsideEVs* Tom Moloughney

Below is Tom's range test of the Tesla model Y:

https://www.youtube.com/watch?v=8zMHNKCJu4s

Tom has tested numerous *EVs* for their real-world range. Just some of the vehicles he has driven to "zero" charge have been; all the Tesla models, Chevy Bolts, Nissan Leafs, Hyundai Ioniq and Kona, BMW i3s, Lucid Air, Rivian and the VW ID.4. This is in no way a complete list of the autos Tom has "run until they died" and his testing is ongoing.

Tom has become the *YouTube* personality who tests and evaluates the "chargers" used on *EVs*. In his *State of Charge* videos goes into great detail about each unit he reviews, and I would not think of purchasing an after-market charging unit without first watching his video on that model.

Tom may also be seen with other *EV YouTubers* on their channels and offers up practical and useful information in regard the *EV* world which I have always found to be well thought out, accurate and valuable.

*

Out of Spec Motoring, InsideEVs and *RateYourCharge* Kyle Conner

Model 3 Holiday Madness Tesla Road Trip | North Carolina to Florida

https://www.youtube.com/watch?v=469rQhSHV3Q

Kyle does a lot of driving in his *EVs*! I recall him mentioning that he put +100,000 miles on his personal Tesla model 3 in a single year (now with +130,000 on that car). Beside him being just a likeable bubbly kind of guy, Kyle offers up really useful, honest, accurate and valuable information on actual observed ranges seen when testing a wide assortment of *EVs*. He also shares his views and impressions on the various models tested, often going into meticulous detail in regard the tested machines components and ergonomics. Kyle doesn't pull punches when he sees an issue! He's not mean-spirited, he is simply honest and truthful.

His site is a mix of testing, charging information, and road trips as well as about his trials and tribulations when traveling across our nation in an *EV,* along with his Significant Other. I have picked up a lot of solid information from watching Kyle's videos.

*

Out of Spec Dave (Kyle's dad)

My New Tesla Model 3 LFP First Drive Impressions Compared To My Old Tesla Model S!

https://www.youtube.com/watch?v=CRtU6hZ-P0w

A lot of enjoyable, down to earth videos made by Kyle's dad (Kathy, his mom, gets involved as well!). Well worth watching and subscribing to. Dave Conner buys and sells interesting *EVs* on a regular basis, discusses their pros and cons, and shares his entertaining road tripping adventures with the *YouTube* audience.

*

Teslabjorn Live Bjørn Nyland

Model 3 Long Range Dual Motor Range Test;

https://www.youtube.com/watch?v=KJpz5imqW5U

Bjørn has one of the best and most informative series of videos you could want in regard *EVs*, the various models out there and their actual distance they are able to travel on a charge. Bjørn has tested dozens of autos, charging them up to 100% and running them to zero SoC. While many of his tested *EVs* are only available in Europe (Bjørn does most of his videos from his home country Norway) his observations, comments, quips, and dry sense of humor is always worth watching.

One of the most useful bits of information Bjørn offers to his watchers is just how much cold temperatures impacts *EV* range. His being situated in Norway is an asset in this regard!

*

Plug & Play EV Steve Birkett

EV Fast Charging: Electrify America Hits 500:

https://www.youtube.com/watch?v=SWQY0dGrbCc

Electric Vehicles, What About Them?!?

Steve is from the Boston area. He has traveled extensively, operating a number of *EVs*, including his 2017 and 2020 Chevy Bolts and now an Ioniq 5. Steve shares his travel experiences (such as his Boston to Austin and return trip), as well as demonstrating various techniques for dealing with the assorted *DCFC EV* charging stations now available for *EV* travelers. I used one of his recommendations (a ChargePoint location in Rhode Island) when driving from Cape Cod to AZ, which I would have never thought of using except for his having reported on it.

*

News Coulomb Eric Way

Tips for Fast *EV* Trip Times

https://www.youtube.com/watch?v=2tYIHZTsDvg

Eric really knows the Chevy Bolt, having put somewhere north of 150,000 miles on his personal vehicle. He is also knowledgeable in regard many aspects of *EV* life, sharing useful information on hard learned proper and efficient road-trip charging protocols. For those of you in the California area, his videos on *DCFC* units in and around that state will prove most valuable.

*

E for Electric Alex Guberman

Top 10 HUMMER *EV* Hidden & Unique Features

https://www.youtube.com/watch?v=-ZLSHfsNW-k

I enjoy Alex's enthusiasm and humor as well as the diverse information and guests he brings to his site. Alex covers a lot of territory and has many knowledgeable visitors on his program (Sandy Munro and Tom Moloughney are two frequent guests) who share their insight and information with viewers.

*

Transport Evolved Nikki and Kate

Ford e-Transit, BMW iX, Kiwi Nissan LEAF Battery Replacement, Bolt *EV* Urgent Recall

https://www.youtube.com/watch?v=-ZLSHfsNW-k

This is a wide-ranging show offering commentary on assorted *EVs*, the evolving technology involved with these vehicles as well as just about all aspects of the *EV* world.

*

Fullychargedshow Robert Llewellyn

Mazda MX-30 First Drive - Does it have a Perfectly Sized Battery?

https://www.youtube.com/watch?v=3nHDONip0SA

Bob offers up diverse videos on various aspects of electrically powered autos, machines, solar energy, and related subjects. As he lives in the UK most of the autos he reviews are intended for the European market. His videos are lots of fun as Bob is entertaining, enthusiastic, and informative.

*

Munro Live Sandy Munro and Cory Steuben

Model Y E40: Mega Wrap Up Episode - Top 10 Takeaways and Future Plans:

https://www.youtube.com/watch?v=TOrrdqje9Og

Sandy, along with Cory, sort of back doored into the *EV* world. They are both highly experienced engineers (among other things) and are part of a business which (as best I can figure) helps engineer, evaluate and design devices (of all sorts) for manufacturing companies, which includes automobiles. Sandy, Cory, and their team have taken apart (and I mean down to the paint!!) a number of *EVs*, including the Tesla models 3, Y, and even the S-Plaid. His videos explaining the good and bad points of these cars is fascinating to watch. Elon Musk commented (on Twitter I believe) that "Sandy Munro understands engineering."

Although their primary business is with OEMs around the world (the company's reports costs run in the six-figure range) the informal informational style they offer, of getting down to the basics of what the average person interested in machinery and technology might want to know and can understand, is excellent, useful and most entertaining.

I always look forward to a new video from Munroe Live. I don't think there is another video site out there than can offer the depth and degree of information on just how *EVs* are made as does those.

*

All Things EV Sean Mitchell

Do I recommend Tesla after 227K miles (365K km)?:

https://www.youtube.com/watch?v=_OBxDDa8J14

Sean, from the Colorado area, offers useful information regarding the *EV* world. As you can see from the attached video of his Sean has a good deal of experience operating a Tesla model S.

*

Rich Rebuilds Rich Benoit

Building an electric mini cooper on a $5,000 budget

https://www.youtube.com/watch?v=PabBvjOBXR8

Rich had been a great source of information regarding Tesla vehicles until he and that company got into a "tiff." That is a rather long story, so suffice it to say that his site offers information into the tearing down and rebuilding of various cars, including many electric vehicles.

*

EV News Daily Martyn Lee

VW increases to $86 billion spending on *EVs*

https://www.youtube.com/watch?v=qyXJjmAlQRQ

Martyn offers up a good deal of information on the goings on in the *EV* world, which he puts out just about every day. As he is from the United Kingdom there is a European flavor to the reporting. Martyn is a frequent guest on the *YouTube* channel, Inside EVs Forum.

*

Inside EVs Forum Domenick Yoney, Martyn Lee, Tom Moloughney, Kyle Conner, and their guests

We Talk With Munro & Assoc President Cory Steuben, RAM 1500 Rev Debuts

https://www.youtube.com/watch?v=vB4N9Wc6djY

Domenick hosts a forum normally containing three or more guests. Most frequently on the weekly show I've seen Martyn Lee, Kyle Conner, and Tom Moloughney among those partaking in the day's discussion. Understand, the *EV* reporting world is a rather "incestuous" one. I say this not as a criticism, just a recognition that we are at the beginning of a new paradigm of human travel options, and there is a limited base of knowledge out there at the moment, of people who have had real-world, hands-on experience in driving and operating assorted *EVs* under all kinds of conditions.

I look forward to these weekly hour and a half long discussions as to what is current in the *EV* world.

*

BestInTESLA Lars Standridder

Tesla makes NEW records | Porsche Taycan is TOO GOOD | Audi is coming with NEW electric car

https://www.youtube.com/watch?v=XUXZM809vZI

Lars is Danish and his channel, while mostly interested in sharing information in regard Tesla goings-on, covers what else is new and interesting in the field of *EVs*. His is an interesting, informative, and entertaining show.

*

The Electric Viking Sam Evans

https://theelectricviking.com/

Sam is a prodigious producer of informative, insightful *YouTube* videos covering the entire spectrum of *EVs*. He offers up discerning comments on the industry and covers Asia, his home nation of Australia, Europe and the United States. I always look forward to an *Electric Viking* program.

*

Richard P. Rosenthal

Tested Ranges of Assorted EVs

I've collected a number of range tests performed by the individuals indicated below, the same tests and people mentioned in my chapter ***Places to Go for More Information.*** A short note/disclaimer; There may be slight variations in the EPA Ranges shown here and the current ranges claimed by the various makers. This is not due to some nefarious goings-on but rather because of updates (some done over-the-air) in the evaluated capabilities of these various *EVs* by their manufacturers.

As indicated below, most of these tests, unless stated otherwise, were performed at 70 mph by the testers mentioned. Again, as I mentioned in the ***Places to Go*** chapter, these individuals are performing a most valuable service for anyone interested in knowing what real-world travel ranges can be expected from whichever *EV* they plan on purchasing.

I cannot emphasize how important this information is for those considering purchasing an *EV*. The labor put in by those who perform these tests require long hours and real dedication. Not only are the tested *EVs* brought up to 100% SoC, these vehicles are then driven at 70 mph until the SoC is down to 0%! This is a time-consuming and tedious process.

Once the range test is completed the *EV* is then plugged in to either a Tesla Supercharger or a *DCFC* station and brought back up to 100% SoC. This is done while the tester videos the process, recording information which can then be shared with their viewers.

Thus you now know not only what you can expect for the real-world range of a particular *EV* but of equal importance how quickly (or slowly...) that model car charges back up.

In the United States, as I stated earlier, the two main individuals who perform this valuable service are Kyle Conner and Tom Moloughney. In Europe such tests are conducted primarily by Bjørn Nyland.

I urge you to subscribe to their various channels on *YouTube*.

Electric Vehicles, What About Them?!?

EV Range Tests @ 70mph (Most Generally)

TM=Tom Moloughney	KC=Kyle Connor	(?)=conflicting numbers
BS=Ben Sullins	BN=Bjørn Nyland	

Unless otherwise noted *EVs* were driven from 100% SoC to 0% SoC.

90kph=56mph   120kph=75mph

Tests shown by year performed. Not always in the order conducted.

2020

EV	Date	Tester	EPA Range	Tested Range
Bolt '20	5/20	TM	259	218
Bolt '20	5/20	KC	259	229
Hyundai Kona '20	6/20	TM	258	245
Hyundai Kona '20	5/20	KC	258	229
Hyundai Ioniq '20	6/20	TM	170	170
LEAF SL+ '20	5/20	TM	215	185
Tesla 3 LR '19	6/20	TM	353	289
Tesla M Y LR '20	7/20	TM	326	275
Tesla M Y LR '20	10/20	BS	326	252
Tesla M Y LR '20 (hot weather test/120*f*)	7/20	KC	326	253
Tesla Model S Raven (90kph/56mph)	5/20	BN	400	385
MINI Cooper SE (90kph/56mph)	4/20	KC	96	132
Audi E-Tron (21" wheels)	9/20	KC	204	189
Jaguar I-Pace EV320 (120kph/75mph/winter)	12/20	BN	227(?)	199
Porsche Taycan 4S (93kWh battery/90kph/68*f*)	8/20	BN	203	360
Porsche Taycan 4S (93kWh battery/120kph/68*f*)	8/20	BN	203	264
Porsche Taycan 4S (70mph/21" wheels)	12/20	KC	203	278

EV	Date	Tester	EPA Range	Tested Range
Polestar 2 (93kph/58mph)	8/20	BN	233	270
Polestar 2 (120kph/75mph)	8/20	BN	233	189

*

2021

EV	Date	Tester	EPA Range	Tested Range
Mercedes EQS 580 (58mph/40*f*)	12/21	BN	350	317
Mercedes EQS 580 (75mph/40*f*)	12/21	BN	350	251
Porsche Taycan 4S (70mph~21" snows/14*f*)	2/21	TM	203	213
VW ID.4 (70mph/40*f*)	3/21	TM	250	234
Porsche Taycan (70mph)	3/21	KC	225	293
Ford Mach-E LR (70mph/70*f*)	4/21	TM	270	286
Tesla 3 LR '21 (80*f*)	5/21	TM	353	310
Porsche Taycan Turismo (70mph~21"/86*f*)	5/21	TM	unk	246
Porsche Taycan Turismo (70mph~21" wheels/86*f*)	5/21	TM	unk	246
Polstar 2 (70mph/67*f*)	5/21	TM	222(Hwy)	226
Ford Mach-E (Stnd Range/85*f*)	7/21	TM	211	226
Ioniq 5 AWD (58mph/79*f*)	7/21	BN	244(Hyundai)	286
Ioniq 5 AWD (75mph/79*f*)	7/21	BN	244(Hyundai)	180
Ford Mach-E Route 1 (70mph/100*f*)	8/21	KC	300	287
VW ID.4 Pro (70mph/89*f*)	8/21	KC	260	229

Electric Vehicles, What About Them?!?

EV	Date	Tester	EPA Range	Tested Range
Polstar 2 Performance (70mph/70*f*)	8/21	KC	233	221
Tesla M S Plaid (21" wheels, 70*f*)	10/21	TM	341	300
Porsche Taycan 4 (70mph/19"/64*f*)	10/21	KC	215	251
Porsche Taycan RWD (70mph/61*f*~70*f*)	11/21	TM	240	297

*

2022

EV	Date	Tester	EPA Range	Tested Range
Tesla 3 SR LFP (58mph/25*f*/Winter Tires)	1/22	BN	253	251
Tesla 3 SR LFP (75mph/25*f*/Winter Tires)	1/22	BN	253	180
Ioniq 5 Limited AWD (70mph/30*f*/20" wheels)	2/22	TM	256	193
Ioniq 5 AWD (70mph/60*f*/19" wheels)	2/22	KC	256	227
Mini Cooper (70mph/66*f*/17" wheels)	2/22	TM	114	103
Mercedes EQS (Mid 60s*f*/21" Wheels)	3/22	KC	350	344
Jaguar I-Pace (Cold WX/22" Wheels)	3/22	TM	234	195
Kia *EV* 6 (Low 70s*f*/77 kWh battery)	3/22	KC	274	254
Tesla 3 Performance (106,000 miles/60~50*f*/12% range loss)	3/22	KC	310	246
Rivian R1T 20" All Terrain wheels/135kWh bat/50*f*	3/22	KC	314	289
BMW M3 Performance (72*f*)	4/22	KC	280	???
Porsche Taycan RWD (70*f*)	5/22	KC	214	200

EV	Date	Tester	EPA Range	Tested Range
Rivian R1T (135kWh battery/20" Wheels)	5/22	TM	270	254
Ford F150-E (131kWh useable battery/Platinum model)	6/22	KC	?	260
BMW*i*-4M (AWD/19" Wheels)	6/22	TM	239	227
KIA EV6 GT AWD (70*f*/20" Wheels)	7/22	TM	265	245
Porsche Taycan RWD ('23 model/80s*f*/New Software/19" Wheels)	8/22	TM	225	305
Genesis GV60 (83*f*)	8/22	KC	235	235
Tesla X LR (20" Wheels/90~100*f*)	9/22	KC	351	331
Bolt 2022 (80s*f*)	9/22	TM	259	260
GM Hummer 1st Edition	9/22	TM	329	343
Lucid Air GT	10/22	KC	516	435
Nissan Ariya (58mph/50*f*/FWD/87kWh Bat.)	10/22	BN	233	278
Nissan Ariya (75mph/46*f*/FWD/87kWh Bat.)	10/22	BN	233	191
Rivian R1S (64*f*/4-motor/135kWh Bat./All terrain tires)	11/22	KC	316	287
GM Hummer 1st edition (35*f*/All terrain tires)	12/22	KC	316	218

*

2023

EV	Date	Tester	EPA Range	Tested Range
Tesla MS Plaid (58mph/46*f*/Custom tires & wheels)	2/23	BN	348	352
Tesla MS Plaid (75mph/46*f*/Custom tires & wheels)	2/23	BN	348	255
Ford Mach-E GT (40*f*/20" wheels/98kWhh battery/dual motor)	3/23	KC	270	234
KIA EV6 GT AWD (40*f*/21" wheels/77kW battery/dual motor)	3/23	KC	206	217

Electric Vehicles, What About Them?!?

2023

EV	Date	Tester	EPA Range	Tested Range
Nissan Ariya Platinum+ (mid-60*f*/AWD/87kWh battery/20" tire)	4/23	KC	272	240
Tesla MY LR AWD (Hertz Rental/mid-70*f*/20" wheels)	4/23	KC	318	286
Ford Mach-E AWD (mid-60*f*/20" wheels/Extended Range Battery)	4/23	TM	270	285

Car and Driver 75 mph *EV* Range Test

The range tests shown below come from those performed by *Car & Driver*. This auto journal conducts their *EV Highway Range Test* at 75 mph, which they believe (and I concur) is a realistic way to evaluate the real-world ranges of electric vehicles. Their testers will, from time to time, have a passenger in their tested vehicles as well as conduct their testing year-round.

One other comment. The reader should be aware that at a highway speed of 75 mph it would be prudent to expect a reduction (dependent on vehicle) in actual highway distance attainable in a given *EV* to be reduced by from 10% on the low end to well over 40% on the high end of EPA rated range. The Audi e-Tron GT being the exception with that vehicle demonstrating a spot-on range estimation. The Porsche Taycan was another *EV* which showed a very accurate range estimation.

Note: EPA range shown is combined highway/city range

EV	2021 Models	Hwy Range Test EPA/*C&D Tested*
BMW i3		153/*–90*
Hyundai Ioniq Electric SE		170/*150*
Volkswagen ID.4 Pro		250/*210*
Tesla Model Y LR AWD		326/*220*
Tesla Model 3 LR AWD		353/*230*
Tesla Model S LR		402/*320*
Tesla Model S Plaid		348/*280*
Ford Mustang Mach-E 4X GT		260/*220*
Audi e-Tron/e-Tron S Sportback		212/*190*
Volvo XC40 Recharge Twin		223/*150*
Nissan Leaf S Plus		226/*180*
Porsche Taycan 4S Battery Plus		227/*220*
Jaguar I-Pace		234/*170*
Audi e-Tron GT		238/*240*
Kia Niro EV EX FWD		239/*180*

Electric Vehicles, What About Them?!?

EV 2021 Models	Hwy Range Test EPA/***C&D* Tested**
Hyundai Kona Electric SEL FWD	258/***160***
Polestar 2	265/***200***
Ford Mustang Mach-E	305/***250***

EV 2022 Models	Hwy Range Test EPA/***C&D* Tested**
Mazda MX-30	100/–***70***
Audi e-Tron (2023)	222/***190***
Nissan Leaf S-Plus	226/***180***
Chevy Bolt EUV	247/***190***
Polestar 2 (2023)	270/***200***
Rivian R1T	314/***220***
Tesla Model Y LR AWD (2022)	330/***220***
Ford F-150 Lightning	274/***230***
Tesla Model 3 LR AWD (2022)	358/***230***
Kia EV6	274/***230***
Tesla Model S LR (2022)	405/***320***
~CA Route 1 RWD (2023)~	312/***???***

*

Edmunds *EV* Range Tests

The auto site Edmunds does regularly updated *EV* range tests. *EVs* are driven approximately 60% city, 40% highway. Here is the link:

https://www.edmunds.com/car-news/electric-car-range-and-consumption-epa-vs-edmunds.html

The list (of just a few of the tested *EVs*) may be seen below, with figures as reported by Edmunds:

EV 2021 Models	Hwy Range Test EPA/***Edmunds***
Ford Mustang Mach-E *(Stnd Range)*	230/***264***
Ford Mustang Mach-E	260/***272***

(GT Performance)
Ford Mustang Mach-E   305/*344*
(CA /Route-1)
Tesla Model 3 LR AWD   353/*345*
Tesla Model S Plaid   348/*345*
Tesla Model Y   326/*317*
(LR AWD)
VW ID.4   260/*288*
(Pro)
VW ID.4   240/*272*
(Pro S Dual Motor)
Polestar 2   233/*228*
(Performance)

EV	2022 Models	Hwy Range Test EPA/*Edmunds*
Hyundai Kona Electric		258/*308*
Hyundai Ioniq 5		256/*270*
(Limited Dual Motor)		
Audi e-Tron GT		232/*285*
Rivian R1T		314/*317*
Lucid Air Dream		520/*505*
Ford F-150 Platinum		300/*331*
Mercedes EQS 450+		350/*422*
Mercedes EQS 580		340/*381*
Kia EV6 RWD		310/*323*
Kia EV5 GT-Line Dual Motor		274/*283*
Polestar 2 LR Single Motor		270/*289*
Polestar 2 LR Dual Motor		249/*288*
Porsche Taycan (20" Wheels)		225/*286*
Porsche Taycan (21" Wheels)		215/*250*
Audi RS e-Tron		232/*285*
Chevy Bolt		259/*278*
Hyundai Ioniq 5 Dual Motor		256/*270*
Tesla Model Y Performance		310/*256*
Nissan Leaf Plus		215/*237*
Toyota bZ4X (2023)		242/*227*

Electric Vehicles, What About Them?!?

Charging Speeds of Various EVs

The fastest way to road travel in an EV

*

I have listed the charge speed of the various model *EVs* by year and manufacturer. Some of the indicated numbers are estimates as I've taken the information from the videos of the various testers and the charging of *EVs* is generally presented as a rapid flow of information.

The primary sources of information the below data comes from are the *YouTube* videos of:

TM=Tom Moloughney   KC=Kyle Connor   *BN=Bjørn Nyland

*Some of Bjørn's tests were not timed, so were omitted.

I've limited the testing results to those from these three guys for the simple reason that they perform these tedious and time-consuming tests in as consistent and professional a manner as is humanly possible. Those of us in the *EV* world (at least us nerds...) owe those three our thanks for taking the time to do this testing in the expert manner as is performed by them.

Most of the tests conducted by them are from 0% to 100% SoC. I first show charge speeds from 0% to 70% as this is a more practical number for most *EV* users to consider. In addition I tried to include the time it takes to get to the full 100% SoC if this was done by the testers.

I limited the years of testing conducted to no earlier than 2021 as too much in the *EV* world has changed for it to be of much utility for readers for me to check out the earlier tests. In addition I've included only vehicles available in North America.

The chargers used were capable of delivering mostly either 150kW, 250kW or 350kW of power. Bjørn's testing was all done in Europe of course, at various fast charge and Supercharger sites there.

Richard P. Rosenthal

Charge rates will be negatively impacted by cooler temperatures. I've included a number of cold weather tests to demonstrate this fact.

In any case you would be well advised to check out the videos of these three testers, especially if there is a particular *EV* you are interested in purchasing.

Keep in mind, it takes as long to charge from 0% SoC to 80% SoC as from 80% SoC to 100% SoC!! Going beyond charging to more than around 70% SoC when you travel makes little sense.

*

The charge sites used in the data shown were:

EA = Electrify America   *Ion* = Ionity (European)   *SC* = Supercharger

*

2021

EV	*Date*	*Tester*	*Site*	*Fm/To*	*Time Min*
Ford Mach-E (AWD 99kWh)	3/21	KC	EA	0%/70% 0%/100%	42 152
Polstar II "	9/21	KC	EA	0%/70% 0%/100%	39 121
Polstar II "	5/21	TM	EA	0%/70% 0%/**90%**	40 63
Audi E-Tron GT (European charger)	10/21	KC	?	0%/70% 0%/100%	16 58
Audi E-Tron GT (85kWh European charger)	12/21	BN	?	0%/70% 0%/**97%**	15 66
Kia EV6 (77kWh)	9/21	KC	Ion	0%/70% 0%/100%	20 48
Hyundai Ioniq 5 "	7/21	BN	Ion	0%/70% 0%/100%	14 44
Mercedes EQS (107kWh)	12/21	BN	Ion	0%/70% 0%/100%	25 60
Tesla M3 (LR/V3 SC)	5/21	TM	SC	0%/70% 0%/100%	26 63
Tesla MY	7/21	KC	SC	0%/70%	24

Electric Vehicles, What About Them?!?

EV	Date	Tester	Site	Fm/To	Time Min
(LR AWD)				0%/100%	99
Tesla S Plaid	9/21	KC	SC	0%/70%	25
"				0%/100%	83
VW ID4	3/21	KC	EA	0%/70%	32
(82kWh)				0%/100%	66
VW ID4	9/21	TM	EA	0%/70%	33
(82kWh)				0%/100%	+64
Porsche Taycan	11/21	TM	EA	0%/70%	16
"				0%/100%	+60
Porsche Taycan	2/21	TM	EA	0%/70%	25
(2020 4S~Cold WX)				0%/**90%**	37
Lucid Air	11/21	TM	EA	0%/70%	17
(2020 4S~Cold WX 350kWh site)				0%/100%	122

2022

EV	Date	Tester	Site	Fm/To	Time Min
Hyundai Ioniq 5	2/22	KC	EA	0%/70%	23
(77kWh~Cold WX)				0%/100%	49
Tesla M3 SR	1/22	BN	Ion	0%/70%	24
(58kWh~Cold WX)				0%/**90%**	44
Tesla M3	2/22	BN	?	0%/70%	25
(LG 82kWh~Cold WX)				0%/**90%**	38
EV	62/22	BN	?	0%/70%	15
(Cold WX~Europe)				0%/**97%**	38
Lucid Air Dream	2/22	TM	EA	0%/70%	34
(150kWh site)				0%/100%	88
Rivian R1T	3/22	KC		314	289
(20" All Terrain tires/135kW bat/50*f*)					

Richard P. Rosenthal

Road Trips We've Taken

The next few chapters of the book will be about some of the longer *EV* trips my wife and I have gone on. I have them shown in the book from most recent to "oldest" as the charging infrastructure is continuously changing (for the better), both for the Tesla brand of *EVs* as well as for those using the *DCFC* system may be seen (we use an adapter).

As this is the Six Edition of my *EV* book I've added our most recent trip from Cape Cod to Green Valley Arizona, with a stop in Scottsdale to pick-up our new Tesla model 3 Standard Range (SR LFP battery type). While the trip was uneventful the story behind it I thought interesting.

I hope you enjoy reading about our little adventures.

Note: Below is the little trip log I published. A notepad would do just as well, but I found my compact *EV Trip Log* works best for us, keeping all the relevant info in one place. As I self-publish my books, creating this little guy was pretty simple. It's available at *Amazon* (type in *EV Trip Log* and my last name):

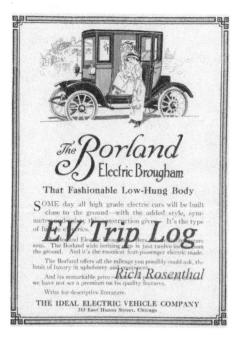

The actual Cover Color of the Trip Log is Sepia

Electric Vehicles, What About Them?!?

Arizona to Cape Cod~Tesla Model Y~2842 Miles (May 2nd~7th 2023)

I would have liked to tease you with some suggestion that this six-day trip entailed numerous death-defying adventures while taking one of those new-fangled *EVs* from AZ to Cape Cod. But I'd be fibbing. The trip was absolutely uneventful (dare I say boring, but in a positive way!). All twenty-four (24) Superchargers used worked perfectly, our Tesla model Y performed flawlessly, the motels were comfortable and the trip was otherwise unremarkable.

The route we took had us driving from Green Valley AZ (south of Tucson), east to Deming NM, then north to Albuquerque, due east till around Pennsylvania then through New York, over the Bear Mountain Bridge, through Connecticut, past Rhode Island and then on to Massachusetts and Cape Cod.

The actual roads driven:
10>25>40>44>55/70>119/22>99/80>81>84>90>495>25/6

Just a few general observations:

- We used this "northern" route, trying to keep away from cities to the extent possible. One headache we had was when traveling through St. Louise Missouri. The confusing and twisting mix of major roads there gave me some white knuckle time.
- Eating on the road. We experimented with purchasing sandwiches for our nightly meal. Much lighter fare than if we had eaten at local restaurants and we found we both felt much better during the trip forgoing eating out at the end of each day's ride.
- The Tesla Supercharger infrastructure continues to impress us. Solid and reliable are the two words which best describes this system. We only came up two locations which were "crowded." None the less, we never missed driving to an open charger. In State College Pennsylvania our luck was to stop in at the Supercharger there (nice place by the way) on

graduation day! There was one open slot, which we took, but others had a short wait as people charged up and departed the location. As this was a 250 kW V3 site, everyone was receiving max power, so things moved along nicely.

The charging infrastructure is expanding out at an impressive rate. There was never a time we had a concern about locating a Supercharger. Indeed, most of the time we picked and chose which places to stop as we wished. Things in the *EV* world are indeed looking up!

Shamrock Texas. Cute small town. Charged here several times.

Twenty-four (24) Superchargers were used during trip which cost $308 dollars. Around 11¢ a mile.

An *ICE* auto, getting 25 mpg, with fuel at $3.70 per gallon, would have cost around $420 dollars.

What follows are the boring basic stats from this road-trip.

Electric Vehicles, What About Them?!?

Arizona to Cape Cod ~ 24,403 miles to 27,245 miles (SC=Supercharger)

	Charger	Stop Time	Fm/To SoC	
Day One fm~to: AZ/Santa Rosa NM				24,403~24,987 miles (584)
1-	SC	6 min	59%~76%	
2-	SC	24 min	23%~79%	
3-	SC	15 min	16%~65%	
4-	SC	13 min	31%~67%	
5-	SC	? min	23%~79%	
Day Two fm~to: Santa Rosa NM/Stroud OK				24,987~25,478 miles (491)
1-	SC	30 min	23%~90%	
2-	SC	14 min	49%~79%	
3-	SC	13 min	35%~67%	
4-	SC	10 min	41%~55%	
Day Three fm~to: Stroud OK/Collinsville IL				25,478~25,947 miles (469)
1-	SC	18 min	30%~74%	
2-	SC	10 min	45%~61%	
3-	SC	15 min	23%~61%	
4-	SC	15 min	22%~30%	
Day Four fm~to: Collinsville IL/Cambridge OH				25,947~26,445 miles (498)
1-	SC	13 min	27%~62%	
2-	SC	? min	33%~90%	
3-	SC	26 min	35%~87%	
4-	SC	19 min	19%~67%	
Day Five fm~to: Cambridge OH/Middletown NY				26,446 ~26,920 miles (474)
1-	SC	? min	20%~76%	
2-	SC	22 min	28%~81%	
3-	SC	15 min	28%~65%	
4-	SC	23 min	38%~82%	
Day Six fm~to: Middletown NY/Cape Cod MA				26,920 ~27,245 miles (325)
1-	SC	7 min	40%~57%	
2-	SC	14 min	22%~66%	
3-	SC	30 min	32%~89%*	

*Food shopping in Orleans MA. Didn't really need a charge.

Richard P. Rosenthal

Cape Cod to AZ to Pick-Up a Tesla Model 3 SR LFP
~2925 Miles
(August 2022)

This chapter is going to be a bit different. We "normally" make an AZ~Cape Cod~AZ Tesla trip each year, trying to get to the Cape by late May or early June. This season (in point of fact on April 1st) we had ordered a Tesla model 3 Standard Range (SR), which uses the LFP (lithium/ferrous or iron/phosphate) battery technology. The story becomes a bit more complex from this point on.

<u>The Battery</u>

There are, at present, two main types of motive battery being used in *EVs*; the so-called ternary type and the LFP variety. The ternary form refers to a battery containing, generally, metal elements of; nickel, cobalt, manganese, or aluminum, which is used as a positive electrode in a ternary lithium battery. The various materials are required for the chemistry to do its magic.

The LFP format uses, beside the obligatory lithium, ferrous metal (iron) as well as phosphate. Other chemistries are being developed as I write this which will likely be included in LFP batteries down the road, and which are designed to enhance the power density of this variety of motive battery.

There are advantages and disadvantages to both types of battery.

First the good news in regard the LFP battery:

- ➢ LFP batteries are substantially cheaper than ternary batteries to manufacture, using less expensive (and easier to source) basic materials in their manufacture (iron is pretty cheap after all!).
- ➢ These batteries are tough. They are reluctant to catch fire, even when treated very badly, say should they become punctured.
- ➢ They are quite long lived. Such a chemistry permits the honest claim of the "million-mile" battery.

> They may be routinely safely charged to 100% State of Charge (SoC), unlike the ternary format, which, except when using the vehicle for a long trip, ought to be kept to no more than at the 80% SoC level.

The downsides of such a chemistry are:

The LFP chemistry does not permit as dense storage of energy as does the ternary style. While the ternary type has an energy density of around 200Wh/kg the LFP kind is somewhere around 150Wh/kg. Yes, I'm being vague here, as this is a moving target. I am aware that research is ongoing which will raise both types of batteries in regard their ability to store electrical power. Some companies are now claiming that their LFP batteries can reach from 200Wh/kg to 230Wh/kg, without losing any of their inherent benefits.

Ternary batteries may well reach the 300Wh/kg level in the near future.

There are a number of other considerations differentiating the two types of motive battery. The ternary can release more of its energy when the temperature drops and there are differences in charging speeds between the two types.

Permit me to sum this up (before your eyes glaze over); LFP batteries tend to be somewhat safer (more fire resistant), have a longer useful life and are more tolerant to high temperature concerns. Ternary batteries are lighter in weight, possess a higher charging efficiency, and are less sensitive to lower temperatures (especially when its below freezing).

On to the story. My wife and I ordered the Tesla M3 SR April 1st. At this time in Tesla's history their vehicles were in serious demand. Depending on the model desired a year's wait was not unusual once you placed your order.

We started getting various, and ever changing, estimated delivery dates (EDD). As we were in southern AZ when the car was ordered, where we would have to be to pick the vehicle up when it was ready, we were in a bit of a bind. My wife and I wished to go to our Cape

Cod place, but we had to put the MA trip off in anticipation of the arrival of the new Tesla.

To further complicate the matter, a person may defer (or put on hold) the acceptance of their ordered Tesla ONE TIME. If the vehicle cannot be picked-up after the second notice of availability then it goes on to the next person.

Finally, by May, after seeing all the date movements putting the EDD further and further out (by then there had been six changes!) we opted to take a chance and head to the Cape in early June. We thought that we'd be safe and that the ordered vehicle wouldn't be available until the Fall.

Well, that's not how it worked out! Come early August and we were notified that the VIN for our car was in! At that point in time there was no way we could get back to AZ for the pick-up so we deferred the purchase. The next EDD we were given was sometime around November. No problem we thought.

The EDD continued to keep on changing. It eventually showed a range of dates from the end of August to early September. At that point we decided we had better head out to AZ a little early, just in case. So, we left on Wed, August 24th, planning a six-day ride in our Tesla model Y back to AZ.

TWO HOURS into the FIRST DAY of the six-day long trip to AZ we receive our latest VIN notice (this means the car was now there!!!!). You can't make this stuff up. Our hearts sank. None the less, we did our phone calls on the road for the required insurance as well as paid for the car with a push of the button (we had the money already in an account Tesla has access to). Tesla does make buying one of their cars quite simple!

Once those formalities had been completed we were required to then opt for a pick-up date (we were given only a three-day window. I had heard it was normally four days.), and chose Monday, the 29th at 3PM (the final day of the trip, and the latest hour available!).

Electric Vehicles, What About Them?!?

Well, being neurotic, which I assure you comes from my wife's side of the family, I had preplanned a four-day, a five-day and a six-day trip to AZ. Just in case. I only made reservations at motels for the first three days of the trip prior to leaving, again, just in case... Fortunately these precautions were not really needed. So, instead of making a left turn when by Albuquerque NM we simply kept on heading due west!

Wife filling up the Tesla at an Electrify America station.

Thus it was that on Monday morning (8/29) we were up at 4AM in Gallup NM and heading out for Scottsdale AZ (where the great unwashed from Tucson at that time had to go to get their Teslas. This has been changed to Tucson for Tesla new car pick up now.). My wife and I arrived at the Tesla facility around 10AM or so, five hours early! We had no hassle with our showing up early. Indeed, the folks there were most helpful.

Spouse checking to make sure Tesla included a battery with the car.

Well, the bottom line is, the car is beautiful. Once the paperwork was finished (which took just a few minutes) I drove the model 3 while the wife took the model Y down to our home in Green Valley.

At any rate, that's our story and we're sticking to it!

*

Boring Stats:

There were no issues with charging the entire six-day trip, so I've kept the data here quite simple:

We left Cape Cod on Wednesday, August 24, 2022 and arrived back home in Green Valley AZ on Monday, August 29th. The length of this road trip was 2,925 miles.

Electric Vehicles, What About Them?!?

During the six days we used the following number of fast chargers:

Superchargers=   17

*Electrify America=   5

*We have an adapter which permits us to access any (literally any) *DCFC* station in the nation. I write about this unit in the chapter on our June 2022 trip from AZ to Cape Cod:

All charging sites worked fine. We expected this from the Tesla system and were pleasantly surprised as to how the *EA* units functioned.

<u>Charge Times During Trip</u>

Below is an overview of how long each "fast charge" stop took for each of the six days of travel.

EA=Electrify America, SC=Supercharger, SoC=State of Charge

	Charger	Stop Time	Fm/To SoC	
Day One fm~to: Cape/Carlisle PA				19,831~20,336 miles (494)
1-	EA	? min	38%~62%	
2-	SC	13 min	54%~78%	
3-	SC	10 min	50%~71%	
4-	SC	16 min	26%~70%	
End Day BW Carlisle PA				
Day Two fm~to: Carlisle PA/Greenfield IN				20,336~20,845 miles (509)
1-	SC	26 min	18%~83%	
2-	SC	18 min	53%~84%	
3-	SC	16 min	25%~68%	
End Day Fairfield Inn, Greenfield IN				
Day Three fm~to: Greenfield IN/Springfield MO				20,851~21,347 miles (496)
1-	EA	15 min	33%~65%	
2-	SC	25 min	32%~84%	
3-	SC	12 min	38%~67%	
End Day BW Springfield MO				

Charger	Stop Time	Fm/To SoC
Day Four fm~to: Springfield MO/Shamrock TX		21,347~21,802 miles (455)
1- SC	23 min	26%~77%
2- EA	18 min	57%~83%
3- SC	15 min	19%~61%
4- SC	? min	19%~71%
End Day Sleep Inn Shamrock TX		
Day Five fm~to: Shamrock TX/Gallup NM		21,802~22,332 miles (527)
1- SC	13 min	40%~69%
2- EA	25 min	22%~81%
3- SC	18 min	57%~88%
4- SC	18 min	39%~76%
5- SC	27 min	20%~78%
End Day BW Gallup NM		
Day Six fm~to: Gallup NM/GV AZ		22,334~22,756 miles (422)
1- SC	7 min	43%~62%
2- SC	21 min	28%~78%
3- SC	22 min	61%~93%
End Day GV AZ (via Scottsdale Tesla to Pick-up M3)		

Cost of the Trip:

EA= $41.18

Superchargers= $129.71

Total $220.89

Electric Vehicles, What About Them?!?

Arizona to Cape Cod~Tesla Model Y~2800 Miles Using a Tesla CCS Adapter!!
(June 2022)

I had an ulterior motive for penning this chapter. It wasn't just another road-trip, but rather our recent acquisition of a Tesla CCS1 adapter enabling us to use <u>any</u> *DCFC* charging station we wish!!

A web site I frequent, <u>Tesla Motors Club</u>, had an active thread about folks purchasing this unit, an "unobtanium" Tesla CCS1 adapter from South Korea.* I thought it might be a bit of a risk but I sent for one none the less.*

*Now available from Tesla USA!!

The box the unit arrived in.

The unit took all of seven days to get from Korea to my home just south of Tucson Arizona! Talk about efficiency. I have not a clue why Tesla did not offer this interface in the State's sooner. This device enables the Tesla driver to access every fast charger in the nation. When hooked into an *EA* 350kW charger I've seen videos of speeds of over 180kW of electrical energy being delivered to Tesla *EVs*.

We used a website of a company called Harumio for the purchase at the time we ordered ours.

This was required as back then, in order to buy the adapter, one had to go through Tesla in South Korea. They needed to verify that I was a Tesla owner before selling the item. Yeah, kind of weird, but that's Tesla for you.

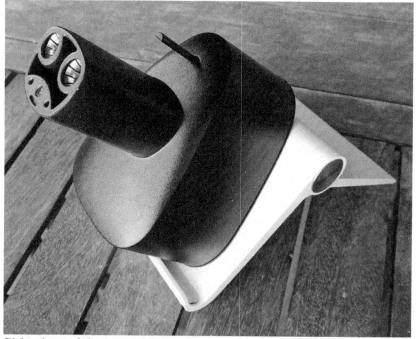

Side view of device. It's simply an interface between the DCFC plug and the Tesla plug.

I wanted this adapter for two purposes:
- ➢ For access to any fast chargers out there, and,
- ➢ For use in the event a Tesla Supercharger site was crowded

Electric Vehicles, What About Them?!?

I planned our latest Arizona to Cape Cod trip with this adapter in mind. Several times during this trip I would be at locations where Superchargers and *EA* sites were co-located. It was at those locations where I'd test the utility of the unit.

To get maximum charging speed in an *EV* the auto's battery requires that the traction battery be heated up prior to charging. Thus the advantage of using co-located charging sites is, I could indicate in the Tesla nav-screen I was heading to a Tesla Supercharger, which would automatically heat up the battery, but then "fool" the car by using the nearby *EA DCFC* site.

***

Well, we made the trip. To make everyone's life a bit simpler I've listed the various *EA* stops where the adapter was used as well as the results of our interaction with each of those sites, in a table format:

*WSC=Walmart SuperCenter

EA Site	Start~End SoC	Max kW Supplied
	Saturday, 6/4/22	
*Deming NM	19%~80%	184kW
Loves, Santa Rosa NM	17%	132kW
Loves, Tucumcari NM	57%~70%	151kW
	Sunday, 6/5/22	
Sam's Club, Amarillo TX	29%~75%	140kW
*WSC, Weatherford, OK	**FAILED TO CHARGE**	
	Monday, 6/6/22	
*WSC, Terre Haute, IN	22%~79%	184kW

Results, Observations and Comments

I had intended to use more than the six *Electrify America* sites we tried. The weather didn't cooperate (lots of rain for a few days) and my wife preferred the simplicity (and reliability) of the Tesla Supercharger system. So I was outvoted...

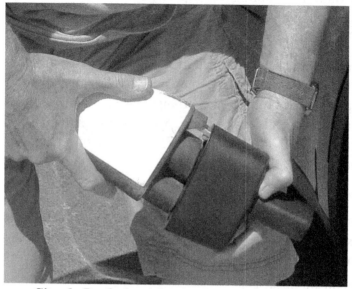

Simply Push the Adapter Onto the DCFC Plug

None the less, I found the use of the CCS1 adapter quite useful. I don't know why Tesla was hesitant to offer the interface in North America at that time. I suspected the corporate view of theirs would eventually come around at some point, and it did.

I had signed up for the four-dollar a month *Electrify America* plus program, which offered lower cost charging prices, and that worked out quite well.

Spouse doing her duty at an Electrify America site "filling up" the Tesla!

Electric Vehicles, What About Them?!?

Cape Cod to Arizona~
3,435 Miles in our Tesla Model Y (October 2021)

This was our third drive going back and forth from Cape Cod to our place south of Tucson Arizona. The first time we did the trip was in our Bolt, this was our second serious drive in our Tesla model Y.

Every time we take such a long trip in an *EV* we learn something. When in our Bolt we had to carefully plan out the entire trip. Had we not done that I'm not sure such a long *EV* journey would have even been possible, using the *DCFC* charging system that was in place in 2019 (such a long time ago...).

With our first long trip in the Tesla (2020) I also carefully planned out the ride. In truth we found that wasn't nearly as necessary. And with this last trip (2021) I planned it out not so much because I had to, but simply because I wished to see where we might be going.

In point of fact I found I only "needed" to figure out where we'd stop for the night when keeping our daily travel legs to around 500 miles. The Tesla on-board navigation system is so good that all I had to do was put in the day's final destination and the system would quickly show me the recommended Supercharger stops to make.

Which I often ignored and would modify on the fly.

Our first two days of travel were spent headed to an old friend (of forty-five years) at his home in Ocean Isle Beach NC. Just under a thousand miles from Cape Cod.

After leaving NC the trip went without a hitch except for two "incidents."

Coming out of San Antonio on a Friday we were hit with a massive rainstorm. Weather had been fine till then, and the rain/lightning came at a really bad place, where multiple roads connected coming out of that city. We had to drive through a "river" at one point which, based on how high the water we saw was coming up to on other cars nearby it had to have reached mid-wheel height. Not fun. Weather was great once out of that mess!

Richard P. Rosenthal

The second event was on day four. We left Boerne TX and our first stop was at Junction TX, a Supercharger site. There were eight charging stations (eight plugs) but only two stations worked! And those at pretty low power. I called Tesla and was told they'd send out a repair crew (it's fixed, I checked a day later with *PlugShare*).

Otherwise all went well on this trip.

*

A word on the most efficient way to road trip an *EV*. Kyle Connor (of *Out of Spec Reviews* among other channels of his) has, literally, hundreds of thousands of *EV* road trip miles under his belt. He knows how to move about long distances in the most efficient manner possible in an *EV*. What Kyle has found is, it's best to charge up to only 50% SoC then immediately set off for the next charging station, aiming to get there with around 5% SoC remaining in your car's main battery pack as the fastest way to travel by *EV*.

I am totally positive that Kyle is correct in his views on this subject. If efficiency and speed of travel is your goal, follow Kyle's recommendation. None the less, I would like to comment that is not how my wife and I handle charging our *EV* as we travel. Permit me to explain.

The difference is, Kyle is a "youngin'!" When I was around twenty years of age I drove with several military buddies from Monterey California to my home in Newark New Jersey, non-stop, in a Rambler! Worked for me then, might not be such a hot idea now that I'm seventy-seven years old!

Neither my spouse nor I are interested in either speed or efficiency of travel in our *EV*. We look for comfort. Therefore we limit our daily rides to around 500 miles and routinely keep our SoC level between +20% and a tad over 70%, not infrequently finding we've put in over 80% of electrical energy in the vehicle at any given Supercharger stop.

Electric Vehicles, What About Them?!?

Using my *EV Trip Log* data, I've put in a stats section following this chapter so you might review how we handled this trip should you wish to do the same.

I repeat myself here; distance travel when in a Tesla is a non-event. Do familiarize yourself with the menu system of the *EV*, I think it only prudent you have some idea as to the distance you'd like to travel during each day's ride, and don't get "cute" by cutting your SoC too close when driving from one Supercharger site to the next.

In short, enjoy the journey. This is not a competition to see how quickly you can get from one place to another!

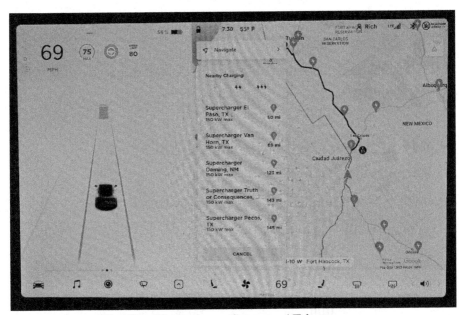

The final leg of our Cape to AZ journey.

The above navigation map shows our route from Route 10/Van Horn Texas and all the way to our home in AZ. The added Supercharger sites are simply additional options offered us should we have desired to utilize them. Once again I feel compelled to state, the Tesla nav screen is beautiful, clear and easy to read, unlike the black and white image I'm compelled to use in this book.

Richard P. Rosenthal

Boring Stats from the Trip

Odometer start:	8,900
Odometer end:	12,335
Total distance:	3,435

Note on Speed of Charging:

I sometimes missed jotting down stop times, so this list is incomplete.

Note on abbreviation; "SC"=Supercharger

Time of SoC start/end of Charging Sessions

Note: Here again I sometimes missed getting the full amount of info, so this list is also somewhat incomplete.

28 Superchargers were used during trip. Cost of Supercharging was $176.36 dollars.

*

Cape Cod to Ocean Isle Beach North Carolina

8,900 miles to 9,879 miles

Length of Stop Minutes	From/To SoC

Day One / 8,900~9,440 miles:	
1- 22 min[1]	44%~85%
2- 21 min	45%~85%
3- 9 min	60%~76%
4- 10 min	36%~60%

[1]Wife went shopping at a Marshall's store

Last stop of day was in Salisbury Maryland

Electric Vehicles, What About Them?!?

Day Two / 9,440~9,879 miles:		
1-	12 min	56%~70%
2-	35 min	25%~83%
3-	19 min	26%~72%
4-	16 min	43%~75%

North Carolina to Arizona

9,995 miles to 12,335 miles

Length of Stop in Minutes		From/To SoC
Day One / 9,995~10,406 miles:		
1-	? min*	24%~86%
2-	9 min	35%~60%
*Watched space launch of "Capt. Kirk" on *YouTube*		
Day Two / 10,406~10,961 miles:		
1-	26 min[1]	52%~89%
2-	20 min	70%~93%
3-	18 min	41%~77%
4-	? min	33%~87%
5-	? min[2]	42%~85%
[1] Wife shopping at Target store		
[2] Two stalls were out, had to wait a bit (Baton Rouge LA SC)		
Day Three / 10,965~11,475 miles:		
1-	22 min	35%~80%
2-	17 min	35%~76%
3-	17 min	31%~74%
4-	23 min	31%~80%

Day Four / 11,475~11,881 miles:		
1-	32 min[1]	44%~58%
2-	37 min[2]	19%~84%
3-	? min	20%~84%
4-	24 min	38%~84%
5-	34 min[3]	38%~93%

[1] Problem at Junction TX SC. Erratic charging. Only two plugs worked and both at partial power. Called issue in to Tesla.
[2] Plugged into the same set of chargers (1A/1B) as another Tesla, both placed at opposite ends of the set of stalls!! Didn't spot the conflict right away.
[3] Talking with another Tesla owner, lost track of time.

Day Five / 11,882~12,335 miles:		
1-	14 min	37%~68%
2-	30 min	32%~89%
3-	8 min	42%~62%

Electric Vehicles, What About Them?!?

Another Cross-Country EV Trip ~ 2,861 Miles in a Tesla Model Y (April 2021)

Disclaimer! This is not a "them vs us" chapter. For reasons which escape me it seems important for some in the *EV* world that there be competition (not infrequently a rather heated one) between those *EVs* which use the *DCFC* system and those using the proprietary Tesla Supercharger system. Well, my wife and I, until recently, drove two different manufacturers *EVs*, enjoyed them both, and valued them for the service and pleasure they gave us.

In short, this chapter is not about taking a shot across anyone's bow!

I will point out the differences I observed when traveling substantial miles in both a Chevy Bolt and the model Y. This is in order to clarify for my readers the distinctions between the two types of charging systems. Which are, in any case, rapidly morphing into operating systems that will be quite similar.

Enough about such things. On to the trip.

*

This is a comparison between our Cape Cod to Tucson trip of October 2020 (in our 2019 Bolt) and our return this April (2021) in a Tesla model Y. This chapter is simply an overview, my just sharing empirical observations on the differences my wife and I found in both the vehicles as well as the two fast charging infrastructures.

The Vehicles

We owned a Chevy Bolt (2019 Premier) and now the Tesla model Y we just drove home in. These are very different vehicles. My wife and I like them both, recognizing that they serve different purposes. The Chevy makes for a perfect commuter car, and we used ours as the "going into Tucson" vehicle as well as for a general runabout. The car is small enough to be agile and easy to park, yet comfortably large enough to have met our storage needs. It was also an enjoyable vehicle to operate. Our Bolt had been stone reliable for all of its

15,000-mile life we owned it. It's rather slow 50kW charging speed is simply dated now and limits this auto's potential travel range.

The Tesla is the better long-distance traveling machine for a number of reasons. It's larger inside, so roomier for both people and "stuff." The Tesla autopilot system works very well, making for a far less stressful day of tedious highway driving. The Tesla mapping system is excellent as well. Their system guides you right to the location of whatever Supercharger you ask it to take you to (or anywhere else you might wish to go for that matter), all the way to your final destination.

For the record we discovered that the Tesla system is so good that preplanning a trip is effectively an affectation, not a necessity. I'll continue to do so as I'm a bit of a nerd (and enjoy the mental exercise of the planning process). But we could just as easily hop into the Tesla at any time and go wherever we wished.

Which brings us to:

Charging Differences

We had some "adventures" when driving in the Bolt when going from Cape Cod to AZ. We were almost stranded twice at *Electrify America* sites the first two days of travel and came really close another day, but managed to drive over 200-miles past one out-of-service charger to another working unit. The Tesla Supercharger system on the other hand, in a few words, simply works. We stopped at twenty-one of those locations (over a 2,800-mile distance trip) and never had an issue. I ought to add that we also drove from Tucson to San Diego CA in the Tesla a month or so earlier, using eight or ten Superchargers at that time and had no issues then as well.

We spoke to a few of the folks we met at Supercharger locations, none had had any negative things to say about the charging system put in place by Tesla.

I am confident that sometime in the future there will be a leveling off of the reliability of *EV* fast charging, with both *DCFC* and Tesla Superchargers working in a similarly consistent and transparent fashion. As of today however my empirically gained view would be that Tesla is the way to go if you intend on doing any significant long-distance driving in an electric vehicle.

I'd like to make it clear that the way we traveled was not particularly "efficient." The least amount of SoC we had upon arriving at a Supercenter was 19%. Most frequently our remaining SoC was over 30%, sometimes more. And because the charging of the Tesla was so rapid that by the time I finished "hitting the head," walking around or chatting with other Tesla drivers parked nearby it was pretty common for our SoC to be in the +80% range. It just happened that way.

Spouse Guarding the Tesla During a Supercharger Session!

Other travelers we met had a different approach. One fellow pulled into a Supercharger site stating (bragging really) that for the last several miles the Tesla was showing "zero" for his SoC. Many of those we spoke with reported being quite comfortable with their SoC being in single digits when coming to the next Supercharger.

My wife and I clearly ascribe to a different philosophy when it comes to fast charging our *EV*!!

Richard P. Rosenthal

<u>Real-world Road Travel Speeds</u>

My wife and I are in our late seventies. We just don't like to sit in a car for much more than a couple of hours at a time. This is my way of saying that our driving style will likely be viewed as inefficient and wasteful of time to many folks. We took six days to travel the 2800-miles, with the maximum day's ride being 541-miles and the shortest being 411. We also didn't drive at any great speed (75 mph cruise max). On the other hand, I'm not sure driving quickly was even all that possible along some of the roads we traveled.

The route we took from Tucson was; 10 to 20 to 30 to 40 to 81 to 78 to 287, over the Tappan Zee/Mario Cuomo bridge, then on to 95 and to the Cape. We found that most people drove at or near the speed limit. Even when wanting to move along a bit it was our observation that we didn't gain much time in trying to jockey in and out of the flow of traffic for that extra five mph of speed. Indeed, in the northeast in particular the speed limits were quite modest, often no more than 65 mph.

Since we were stopping every 150 or so miles anyway, racing to the next Supercharger, then hanging out there to take a break just didn't seem to make much sense.

So, in short, most people would be able to make far better time, as well as stopping at fewer chargers, then was the case with us. I suspect we stopped at around eight or ten more Superchargers than we really had to in order to make this trip. We drove for our comfort, not to make the best time.

As an aside we stayed at five motels along the route, with four having Level 2 chargers available, which was quite handy.

At the end of this chapter I've included a (boring) day by day overview of where we charged, the SoC at each location and the maximum charge rate I observed (which will not be 100% accurate as I've noted charge rates increase with a lower SoC and it's likely I missed seeing some of that taking place).

Electric Vehicles, What About Them?!?

Supercharging Stops AZ to Cape Cod

Info listed by day of trip/miles driven, then Supercharger used with SoC at the start of the charge session and the kW of electricity going into the Tesla. Total miles driven, door to door, was 2861. At the motels we stayed at on days one, two, three and five we had access to Level 2 chargers.

Day 1 541miles	Wilcox AZ 65% SoC @ 95kW	Deming NM 31% SoC @ 136kw	El Paso TX 46% SoC @ 141kW	Van Horn TX 19% SoC @ 136kW
Day 2 454 miles	Midland TX 56% SoC @ 115kW	Sweetwater TX 41% SoC @ 142kW	Cisco TX 39% SoC @ 117kW	
Day 3 459 miles	Texarkana TX 36% SoC @ 146kW	Little Rock AR 27% SoC @ 139kW		
Day 4 411 miles	Dickson TN 39% SoC @ 137kW	Cookeville TN 30% SoC @ 146kW	Knoxville TN 53% SoC @ 66kW	
Day 5 521 miles	Bristol TN 40% SoC @ 142kW	Wytheville VA 37% SoC @ 139kW	Lexington VA 33% SoC @ 141kW	Strasburg VA 34% SoC @ 140kW
Day 6 475 miles	Boontown NJ 42% SoC @ 134kW	Madison CT 46% SoC @ 127kW	Sagamore MA 34% SoC @ 102kW	Orleans MA 33% SoC @ unk rate[1]

[1]This stop wasn't necessary. We decided to do some food shopping prior to getting home and there is a bank of Superchargers at the grocery we stopped at.

***

Richard P. Rosenthal

A Long EV Trip ~ 2,742 Miles in a Chevrolet Bolt (October 2020)

Cape Cod to Green Valley Arizona

There are two primary purposes an *EV* owner can put their battery powered auto to; local use and/or distance travel. I suppose the same might be said of most *ICE* vehicles. None the less, while a compact *ICE* runabout which is used to go back and forth to work might not be ideal for going cross-country, although perhaps being an uncomfortable way to spend long travel days in such a tight space, such a trip could certainly be accomplished. With *DCFC EVs* this may not necessarily be the case. The range of the lower range models of currently available *EVs* could well preclude consideration for such a journey in the first place.

As in all else in the *EV* world this situation is changing rapidly. I say this for two main reasons; the "legs" (range) of *EVs* are getting longer all the time, thanks mainly to developments in the field of battery technology as well as the fact that the charging infrastructure is growing at a rapid rate.

I have alluded to this before in the book, we are at the very beginning of seeing a number of disruptive technologies which are pushing out existing paradigms. The electric vehicle is simply noticeable evidence of several of them. While the undertaking of a long road trip (say around 1,000 miles in an electric vehicle) is of some interest, and worthy of discussion today, in a very few years (certainly in less than five) such travel using an *EV* will be as routine as hopping into the family jalopy and just taking off to wherever one's heart desired.

In October 2020 my wife and I found ourselves on Cape Cod and needed to reposition our Chevy Bolt, a 2019 Premier model, from our home there to our place just south of Tucson Arizona in the small community of Green Valley. We had shipped a car from that home to our other abode some years ago, and the process went smoothly, so that certainly was a viable option. But as I was working

Electric Vehicles, What About Them?!?

on this book about electric cars, I thought what better way to demonstrate the viability (or insanity) of such a trip then by taking an *EV* three quarters of the way across the nation!

A few disclaimers here:

This trip would not have been practical in a *DCFC* equipped *EV* only a year or so prior to this ride. There were simply an insufficient number of rapid charging stations out there for such a journey to have been doable. Could it have been done? Sure. You could also harness up old Dobbin (Dobbin is "old speak" for a horse...) and have made the trek in a buggy. Such a trip would have been about as practical and take about the same amount of time (OK, I'm exaggerating a bit here)!

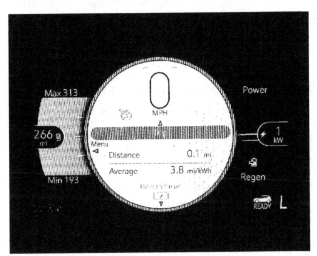

The Bolt Can Have Long Legs!!

An *EV* with sufficiently long range would be needed. Our Bolt has a nominal max-charge range of 238 miles. At modest speeds, and under mild weather conditions (temperature being the main variable) the vehicle can travel quite a bit farther than that. The instrument showing projected range of our Bolt during the start of each day's travel would routinely indicate a range of from over 260 miles to, on occasion, and if we'd driven at prudent speeds the day prior, to just over 300 miles.

As I have discussed earlier in the book there are two primary types of charging infrastructures now in our nation; *DCFC* and Tesla's. The Tesla system has been around for over a decade, goes from coast to coast, requires a simple plug-in to the Tesla vehicle and with no further effort on the part of the driver the auto begins to receive its electrical charge. Furthermore, the computer system in each Tesla is designed to that when you inform the computer where you wish to go, the places you should stop in order to charge successfully to get there are automatically calculated for you. Not only will the car basically take you from charge station (called Superchargers) to station but will inform you as to how many of the plugs are in use at the moment as well as their status. It is a very sleek, user friendly, albeit proprietary, *EV* charging system.

The *DCFC* model is a different animal. Permit me to observe that this system is evolving, and I fully expect the reliability and user interface simplicity of *DCFC* equipped vehicles will match up with the Tesla system sometime in the near future. Not having a working crystal ball handy, I can only report on what is available out in the world as of today.

In other chapters I have mentioned some of the various players in the *EV* charging system. The dilemma *DCFC* users face is that:

Each of the vendors systems require a slightly different protocol in order to get a charge.

Some use RFID cards (Radio-Frequency Identification or the so-called "chips" as seen in most newly issued credit cards ~ ChargePoint for example issues such an RFID card when you join that charging entity), others use such cards as well

NFC symbol Above

or give users the ability to access a charge either through a smartphone app or by touching a suitable smartphone to the electronic sensor on the face of the charging device. The latter is called Near Field Communication (NFC) and permits the transfer of information from one electronic device (or suitably chipped card) to another. Such units are becoming fairly common at many points of payment where the user can simply tap their credit card (or smartphone) against the appropriate symbol at the check-out counter.

Fortunately, most chargers installed now permit the use of the *EV* driver's credit card, albeit at a higher cost than for those who are members of that charging service.

Oh, and one last bit of advice; if you plan on taking your significant other along on a *DCFC* powered trek, they had better be as understanding and patient as my wife!!

*

OK, so here are some take-aways from my wife's and my 2,742 mile road trip in the Bolt, from MA to AZ.

BOLD = Hi-Power-DCFC ~ Number in () = recommended station to use

Day 1 / 490		Day 2 / 475
Home MA		Comfort Inn, PA
120		27 optional
Warwick Park & Ride Rt 117 Park&Ride, Warwick RI		Sheetz 1098 Harrisburg Pike, Carlisle, PA
60		60 optional
Stratford Square 311 Veterans Blvd, Stratford, CT		Hagerstown Valley Mall 17301 Valley Mall Rd, Hagerstown, MD Caution, may need to go to Brugh's for charge next 200 miles
80		130 fm Sheetz Carlisle - 160 fm PA Motel
The Mills at Jersey Gardens 651 Kapkowski Rd, Elizabeth, NJ (3)		Walmart Supercenter 461 W Reservoir Rd, Woodstock, VA (3) Check to see if working!! or use Jack Evans Chev 125 S Royal Ave, Front Royal, VA + 155 to Brugh's
95		160 or 200 if fm Hagerstown!
King of Prussia Mall - Southwest 160 N. Gulph Road, PA		Brugh's Mill Country Store 384 Brughs Mill Rd, Fincastle, VA (4)
85		150
Comfort Inn & Suites 1589 W Harrisburg Pike, Middletown, PA (717) 857-8776		Sam's Club 13249 Lee Hwy, Bristol, VA (3, 4)
		40
		Fairfield Inn and Suites 3078 Hamilton Pl, Johnson City, TN 423-900-8640
		or
		MeadowView Conference Resort & Convention Center 1901 Meadowview Parkway, Kingsport, TN 423-578-6600

Prior preparation and planning were critical. Otherwise you cannot jump into a non-Tesla electric car and have any reasonable hope of successfully making a long distance (five hundred mile plus) trip at this moment in time. In a few years, probably. But not now.

To the left is a sample of one of the "cheat-sheets" I prepared prior to the start of the journey. These were so helpful that I ask you to pay attention to the information contained therein and understand why such a pre-prepared document proved so useful during this trip.

Richard P. Rosenthal

This sheet is for "Day 1" and "Day 2" (there were three pages in total, for the six days of travel) where you will see I have inserted the following information:

<u>Day of trip</u>

- ➢ In order: Start of day to the motel at the end of the day, with its physical address and phone number.
- ➢ The number in bold is the distance between stops.
- ➢ VERY IMPORTANT: Note that I included the actual physical address of each stop. I'll explain why in a moment.

From top to bottom:

The information contained on your information page will show you just how far you have to go from stop to stop. This can be difficult to do "on the fly" when driving along on a multi-thousand-mile ride. The advantage you will have is, if you're 95 miles from the next charger, and you need to put in around 120 or 130 miles of charge to safely get there as shown on the GOM (Guess-O-Meter!), you can be confident that you can "make it" to that destination with some certainty.

Why the physical address? Because sometimes the navigation systems in our cars will not recognize the name of the place you want to go to (the *Electrify America* site at "Brugh's" came out something else every time I tried enunciating it!), or, as with Walmart Supercenters, there may be several Walmart's located around a larger metropolitan area, but only one of them is equipped with an *Electrify America* bank of chargers (as happened on this trip a number of times!). What to do? Simply have the navigation system direct you to the physical location desired and problem solved!

Finally, you will want the phone number of the motel where you desire to be at the end of the day to be handy. I urge you to call in your reservation early in the day. Depending on the season of the year, the time of day and how much travel is going on around you, not doing so might result in you needing to find a different location than the one you planned on staying at. Furthermore, I picked all the motels we stayed at in order to ensure they had complimentary *EV* chargers, so we would start each day at 100% of battery charge. This last precaution worked out well for us.

In total 23 *DCFC* charges were needed on the road during the trip:
- 2 ChargePoint units we used functioned just fine
- 2 *EA* units needed phone assistance and were partial failures (both on day one, in CT and NJ)
- 3 *EA* sites were total failures (day one in PA, day two in VA and day four in AR)
- 16 *EA* chargers worked as they were designed to function

Note, each of the *EA* units used from Hope AR to the final *EA* site in Benson AZ, ten (10) in total, performed perfectly!

Why I counted the need to call in order to get a charge from the two *EA* units as partial failures is because every time I made the call required me to give the person on the other end a string of identifying information. This included:

- Name
- Email
- Phone number
- Last four digits of my credit card

I believe there was one or two other bits of information that was required, but I don't recall what they were at the moment. Think of it this way. Say you were on a long-distance trip and the Mobil station you stopped at to fill up your *ICE* vehicle had the pumps down, and the nearest gasoline station was beyond the range of your car. You call the company for assistance but must first recite this litany of information to the person at the other end in order to get some help. This happened to me three times on the first day of travel, the last problem was unable to be resolved by *EA* staff and we were close to being stranded in Pennsylvania on a Sunday night!

The second day of the trip had us stranded in the vicinity of Fincastle VA (the *EA* site in question was at Brugh's Mill Country Store and had gone down that very day!). The nearest *DCFC* was 150 miles away (Sam's Club, Bristol VA). Fortunately there was a nice Best Western in Troutville, VA quite close by, which had two J1772 chargers and four Tesla destination chargers. It was an agreeable place. The chargers were set up right by the side of the building. Very well done.

On day three we decided to try and make up for some of the lost 150 miles of the previous day. We pushed on to a Comfort Inn in Dickson TN. The four *EA* units we used that day all worked out fine.

Day four had the last problem with *EA* for the entire trip. Our first stop out of Dickson was at a Walmart Supercenter in Forrest City AR. No problem. However, although I had checked every single *EA* charger on the *EA* app that morning, and all were showing they were up and running, while charging in Forrest City I checked the next stop in Little Rock (by this time in the trip I was pretty paranoid). Sure enough it had gone down (it was up later that afternoon, I checked again!) and the next *DCFC* was located over 200 miles away from the site we were at, in Hope AR!

We opted to charge the Bolt to 92% and drive on. The charge time took us one hour (ever watch paint dry...?). We drove no faster than 60 mph to Hope AR, using no AC but with the fan on. It was a long ride...

We got into Hope with 18% remaining in the motive battery. This taught me a lesson. If you really have to, and are aware of the problem before starting out, and the weather is on your side (not too cold out, no rain or strong winds coming at you from the wrong direction) you can really get some miles out of the Bolt.

From Hope AR all the way to Benson AZ every *EA* site worked as advertised. So here's the rub; clearly this is an industry in its infancy. And like the nursery rhyme,

> *When she was good,*
> *She was very good indeed,*
> *But when she was bad she was horrid.*

When *EA* units worked well, and the last ten units were great, you just loved the company. But we needed twenty-three charges...

Electric Vehicles, What About Them?!?

What I took away from the trip

I love electric vehicles. My wife and I have decided that we will never purchase another *ICE* vehicle again. Period. When people ask me questions about *EVs* I answer them as follows. If you want a vehicle for local driving, commuting or such, there is no finer machine than an electric car. However, as of today, if you wish to have a practical auto for distance travel that is electric, the only company's reliable offerings at the moment are from Tesla.

My wife and I really respect the great little car that our Bolt is. We hoped to keep this vehicle for a long time. It was to be driven all over southern AZ. None the less we now have a Tesla model Y for our back-and-forth travels to Cape Cod. And have since picked-up a Tesla model 3 SR.

Might this change someday? No doubt. But I cannot tell you when.

Apps used in Trip Preparation

You must carefully prepare your route prior to setting foot in your non-Tesla *EV*! Had I not meticulously planned out each day's itinerary, putting down on paper (samples at end of thread) every charging station we were to use, including some possible options, the motels we were planning on using, and, most important, the distance between each, we would have had serious problems. That last, distance, was vital. It is difficult to figure out stuff when you are frazzled, angry and upset.

Although I used both *PlugShare* and *ABRP*, I never looked at the printouts from *ABRP* the entire trip. One nice thing I found about *PlugShare* were the users' comments about the specific sites. The information offered was most useful. For example, at one site was a nice motel we stayed at in Pecos Texas, the Best Western Plus Swiss Chalet. I knew they had both Tesla destination chargers and at least one J1772 plug, the type needed for our Bolt. Once there I asked where the J1772 plug was located and the young lady behind the desk waved in a general direction to the rear of the motel parking lot.

I explained that I needed a specific type of plug and she assured me the plug there was for "general use."

Making a rather long story short, her directions led me to a Tesla plug. And when I explained this to her, she argued with me! At any rate the *PlugShare* site informed me as to the specific location of the proper plug (it was at the Best Western motel right next door, which was owned by the same people), and we received a full charge from it for the next leg of our journey.

Another thing, always (always, as never omit this information) put down the <u>physical address</u> of every *DCFC* charging location! "Why?" I hear you ask, when you can just tell Google the name of the location where you want to go and the mapping system will take you to that very place, correct?

Sorry, sometimes that will not work. As mentioned earlier I could not, for the life of me, get the system to recognize the word "Brugh's" (for an *EA* site at Brugh's Mill Country Store in Fincastle VA. That site was down when we got there anyway!). This happened a number of other times when going to different locations during the trip. And if you simply say "Navigate to Walmart" you might well find there are three Walmart Supercenters in that area! And only one of them has an *EA* station. But, as I had printed out the physical location of the sites I wished to travel to, I simply entered the addresses into the Google mapping system and avoided a problem.

As an aside, *EA* placing their *DCFC* stations at Walmart's was a great idea! At most of our stops we had access to clean restrooms, food, sundry items we desired to purchase, whatever we wished. One thing, when we first were going to the various Walmart locations on occasion we had a devil of a time finding the chargers. The wife and I would play a game of "Where's Waldo?" and keep score as to who spotted the "hidden" *EA* stations first.

Electric Vehicles, What About Them?!?

I thought it to be a conspiracy. My wife figured out what the deal was. She noted that the charging stations had always been shrouded (cleverly cloaked) behind a large gray metal wall. Well, that masking "wall" was the enclosure protecting the sophisticated electrical equipment necessary for the operation of the chargers. So we stopped looking for little white rectangles in a sea of autos at Walmart parking lots and looked instead for a hulking Abrams tank size metal enclosure. Easy peasy. Kind of took the fun out of locating the chargers.

One of the carefully placed camouflage walls hiding EA chargers!

After the third day of the trip we discovered that the *EA* chargers we visited were located in really convenient spots (the older sites in the northeast sometimes had us driving quite some distance from the interstates). They were right off the main roads, with easy on and off access. The units in Connecticut and New Jersey that we used were not as convenient to get to. On a few occasions we had to drive quite a distance through small towns to a site. Not bad if you are on a day trip, but if you need to make 500 miles that day, well, not so swell.

We saw a number of other *EVs* at the various chargers. I only spoke to a few of the drivers. One lady had pulled in with an Audi e-Tron. She had 9 miles showing on her GOM. If that station had been down, she would have been camping at Walmart's for the day! I tried to explain to her how she could check to see which *EA* stations were up using their app, but she had no interest in hearing about it.

Folks, the people reading this book are likely intensely interested in electric vehicles. The vast majority of the population view *EVs* as nothing more than cars in which you put electricity instead of gasoline in order to make them go. And they expect the same kind of reliability when arriving at a charging location as they get at their local Citgo. This is not a minor issue.

Another thing we should discuss is, just how practical is multi-thousand-mile *EV* travel at this time? I would argue, save for the Tesla system, we are not there yet. If you look at *PlugShare*, most of our trip had no real-world possibility for finding a *DCFC* between stations of less than 100 or more miles apart! We are in serious need of more charging infrastructure. But most of the people reading this book already know that.

We also had an iPad connected to the Verizon network with us. The iPad proved quite useful. It found us the nearby motel when we were stranded on the second day of the trip. Don't leave home without it...

The *EA* app at the time of this trip was too complex. Permit me to explain. We stopped at two ChargePoint locations, Warwick RI and Greeneville TN. Pulled up to the station, plugged the car in, touched the RFID card to the little symbol on the stanchion and electricity started to flow immediately! Shocking. I thought I was charging at a Tesla location by mistake!

With the *EA* app (as when this trip took place) the following procedures had to be followed (I have set aside several of these screens for your inspection at the end of this chapter):

- Plug your car in
- Open the app (duh)
- You should be automatically signed in. If not, sign in!
- A map will appear
- Touch the little arrow at the top of the app to put you at your current location
- Touch the *EA* symbol on the little map (green lightning bolt in a black dot)
- The site will come up at the bottom of the screen

- ➢ Scroll up and find the charger you are parked by (numbers printed on top!)
- ➢ Touch your station's number in the app
- ➢ The start bar will appear (if the deities are smiling on you that day)
- ➢ Scroll the *EA* symbol on the start bar to the right

The system should recognize your car and initialize (if in a Bolt best hang on and push tight to the plug until the plug grabs firmly to the socket or you may lose the charge).

That is a fair amount of "stuff" to do to start a charge. Especially so if other companies can find simpler ways of performing the task. I sure hope *EA* can eventually work out an easier system to use as well. As this book is being written I am aware that *Plug&Charge* works for certain capable *EVs*.

Note, when you touch on a charger station on the *EA* app information is presented informing you when that station was last used by date and time.

At some *EA* sites there are also RFID contacts so you can touch your phone to activate the charge. Sometimes that will do the trick. Credit card readers are at these sites as well, but if you are enrolled as a Pass + member if you use your credit card you'll be charged as if you weren't.

Oh, yeah, cost of the trip. Around .03 cents a mile. 2,740 miles for around $92 dollars. Those numbers are truthful, but not accurate. For example, the ChargePoint in Warwick RI was free. *EA* was kind enough not to charge me for the two stops that worked the second day of the trip (I think they took pity on me). Thus the actual cost was somewhat more than $92 dollars. Let us call it .04 cents a mile, which I think is a fair estimate.

One last thing about the *EA* app; I listed every single *EA* site I had planned to charge at, for the entire trip, into the app as "Favorites." To do this all you need do is go through the map on the screen, touch on the *EA* symbol at the site you'll be using and, when you touch on the site name, at the bottom of the screen a menu should rise up and the option of clicking on "Favorite" (a heart shaped symbol) will be offered for that site. This saved me a lot of time as I moved along as I checked on each and every site I was headed to before leaving the charging station I was then at.

Thank You Note to My "Staff"

I am fortunate to have, living with me, my book's editor. As I was raised and educated for the first fourteen years of my life in Brooklyn, New York, my failing to master the intricacies of English grammar and syntax is easily explained due to my having gone through the New York City school system.

Fortunately I had the wisdom fifty or so years ago to marry a very bright and competent person who, due to her having gone through the German educational system, has a much better and more nuanced comprehension of my native tongue than I do.

Therefore, I wish to thank my long-suffering wife, Frauke, for the assistance she gave me in correcting my many mistakes in this book's manuscript.

Frauke, in Arizona, by our Jeep

Made in the USA
Middletown, DE
19 May 2023

30568589R00116